Plenty Good Room
The Spirit and Truth of African American Catholic Worship

In truth, I see that God shows no partiality. Rather, in every nation whoever fears him and acts uprightly is acceptable to him.
—Acts 10:34-35

There's plenty good room in my Father's Kingdom.
—Spiritual, "Plenty Good Room"

Secretariat for the Liturgy and
Secretariat for Black Catholics
National Conference of Catholic Bishops

United States Catholic Conference • Washington, D.C.

From 1987 to 1990, the approved plans and programs of the NCCB Secretariat for the Liturgy have included the development of an in-depth reflection on African American worship as a companion document to *In Spirit and Truth: Black Catholic Reflections on the Order of Mass*, a 1987 statement of the Secretariat. *Plenty Good Room: The Spirit and Truth of African American Catholic Worship* was approved by the NCCB Committee on the Liturgy and the Committee for Black Catholics at their June 1990 meetings and is now authorized for publication as a joint statement of the Secretariats for the Liturgy and for Black Catholics.

Monsignor Robert N. Lynch
General Secretary
NCCB/USCC

Cover Art/Text Illustrations: Mr. James Stephenson; Detroit, Michigan
Graphic Designer: Mr. Terrence Curry, SJ; Detroit, Michigan
Consultant: Rev. J-Glenn Murray, SJ; Cleveland, Ohio
Production: Guild, Inc.; Hyattsville, Maryland

This project was funded in part by the ACTA Foundation, Chicago, Illinois; and by the Commission for the Catholic Mission Among the Colored Peoples and the Indians, Washington, D.C.

ISBN 1-55586-385-X

First Printing, September 1991
Third Printing, April 2000

Contents

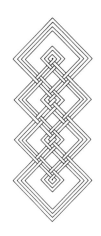

Preface

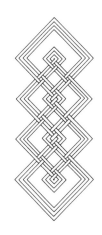

The Black Liturgy Subcommittee, formed by the Bishops' Committee on the Liturgy in 1984, was charged with addressing the liturgical issues and concerns of the African American Catholic community. One issue taken up early by the subcommittee was the adaptation of the liturgy to accommodate the style and eloquence of African American communal prayer. After studying the various styles of celebration found in predominately African American parishes, the subcommittee drafted and, in 1988, published *In Spirit and Truth: Black Catholic Reflections on the Order of Mass* as a secretariat statement. That document presented the options and choices in the Order of Mass that are available to those wishing to marry the richness of the Roman Rite with the genius of the African American culture.

Now, as a companion to that document and in order to continue the dialogue necessary to approach any cultural adaptation of the liturgy, the Secretariats for the Liturgy and for Black Catholics offer *Plenty Good Room: The Spirit and Truth of African American Catholic Worship*. This document lays the theological foundation for cultural adaptation; frames the discussion of the interplay between culture and liturgical celebration; examines the historical, cultural, and religious experience of African Americans; and distills several elements particular to African American worship.

Although this statement has been written with a particular view toward the African American Catholic community, the principles offered, especially in the chapters on "Liturgy and Symbolic Reality," "Liturgy and the Christ Event," and "Liturgy and Culture," are applicable to any culturally distinct community interested in understanding the relationship between culture and religious experience. The final four chapters deal directly with the African American religious experience. The ideas contained in these chapters can also serve as a model for discerning the heritage of a particular group and for discovering ways already available to ritualize appropriate cultural prayer practices.

The Bishops' Committee on the Liturgy is grateful to its Black Liturgy Subcommittee and to the Bishops' Committee

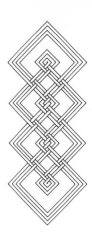

for Black Catholics for the joint effort that has produced this statement. It is but another example of the valuable contribution African American Catholics continue to make to the Church in the United States.

August 28, 1990
The Memorial of
Saint Augustine, Bishop of Hippo

> Most Reverend Joseph P. Delaney
> Bishop of Fort Worth
> (Former) Chairman
> Bishops' Committee on the Liturgy
>
> Most Reverend John H. Ricard, SSJ
> Auxiliary Bishop of Baltimore
> Chairman, Bishops' Committee for Black Catholics

Introduction

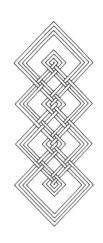

Whatever is genuinely human must echo in the hearts of the followers of Christ.[1] In our day, the Church senses an echo that is becoming ever more intense. Its source is a spiritual heritage that has brought great joy and hope for African Americans for these three-plus centuries of our presence in this land. It is an echo that offers not only joy and hope, for on occasion it has expressed grief and anguish as well. It is an echo that tells a story born of poverty and affliction, and therefore it must be an echo that the Church receives and embraces.[2]

The Church lives in the modern world with a heart that must be ever open to the sounds that voice the joy and hope, the poverty and affliction of humanity. Those sounds are found most eloquently in the cultures of the human family. The *Pastoral Constitution on the Church in the Modern World (Gaudium et Spes)* carefully describes the significance that human cultures have and what they can offer to contemporary society and to the Church itself.[3] There is little wonder that the rediscovery of the sources and processes of the formation of African American culture has begun to influence the Catholic Church in the United States.

There is no place within the life of the Church where the influence of African American culture is to be more profoundly discovered than in its liturgical life. For several decades, Black religious music has had a respected place alongside other indigenous American hymnody in Catholic worship. But more recently, African American art, devotional traditions, styles of preaching and praying, rhythm and tempo at worship services also have begun to influence Catholic liturgy. These elements of culture have brought joy and hope to a great many Catholics, and for some even a degree of grief and anguish. The Black Liturgy Subcommittee of the Committee on the Liturgy of the National Conference of Catholic Bishops is pleased to share *Plenty Good Room: The Spirit and Truth of African American Catholic Worship* with all those who have come to love the joy and hope to be found when the African American religious spirit touches the heart of Catholic worship.

The Bishops' Committee on the Liturgy has prepared this statement for those who wish to reflect more deeply on the Church's encounter with African American culture in its worship. It is issued as a joint statement of the Secretariats for the Liturgy and for Black Catholics to offer important guidance in assessing the subject at hand.[4] The African American culture,

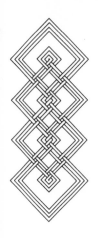

like all human cultures, develops according to processes outside the control of the Church itself. We, therefore, have no desire to judge, limit, define, or control the past or the ongoing development of Black culture—or any other culture for that matter. We would be remiss, however, in failing to address this moment in the history of the Church and in our modern world when the Church has begun to encounter, as perhaps never before, the wonderful presence of the culture of African Americans in its worship. It is too early to draw the types of conclusions that only history will be able to provide in determining the final benefits in the process of liturgical accommodation. But should we wait until that moment when these processes have reached greater maturity, we might well be judged to have been guilty of undervaluing a significant dynamic that is currently making an impact on the Church and promises to do so with ever greater intensity in the future. Seen in this light, our observations are subject to further review and reflection as the liturgical renewal continues—a process not unfamiliar to the entire Church since embarking on the reform of the sacred liturgy.

The members of the Black Liturgy Subcommittee are also aware and respectful of the multicultural diversity embraced by the African American religious heritage. While we might speak in general terms regarding elements of Black culture, we realize that such generalities do not exhaust the complexity of our own heritage. Nonetheless, those dimensions of the African American culture referred to in this statement have achieved a status within Catholic liturgical celebrations, which makes them significant for further reflection. We acknowledge that many of these same elements elicit a variety of opinions within the African American community itself, as well as among members of the Catholic Church at large.

With the personally expressed encouragement of our Holy Father, John Paul II, we are embarking upon this adventure so that all may better understand and preserve our precious African American heritage for the glory of the Church, which stands to continue benefiting from the gifts of our cultural treasures.[5]

Plenty Good Room: The Spirit and Truth of African American Catholic Worship is a companion statement to *In Spirit and Truth: Black Catholic Reflections on the Order of Mass* (Washington, D.C.: USCC Office for Publishing and Promotion Services, 1988). While that former document was far more limited in scope, since it only reviewed the possible areas for cultural adaptation that currently exist in the Order of Mass, *Plenty Good Room* explores the more substantive issues of cultural ad-

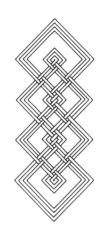

aptation itself and the challenges that worshiping communities face in attempting to achieve such adaptation. Such an exploration must not only be securely rooted in a further examination of the symbolic nature of ritual and the sacred liturgy, but also in its cultural adaptation throughout the centuries and, in particular, in the African American religious experience in the United States. It was the original intention of the Black Liturgy Subcommittee to prepare such a statement, with the hope that it would serve as an exposition of the processes that are occurring in this moment of liturgical adaptation and as a rationale for their fruitful completion.

The entire Church is poised at the present moment, still awaiting greater clarity and direction in evaluating the appropriateness and effective accomplishments of cultural adaptation for a host of communities and peoples all encountering the Roman Rite with their cultural individuality. There are those who desire more specificity in this delicate yet difficult task. The Church, drawing upon the wisdom gained from other such moments in its almost two thousand year history, is careful to avoid making a too hasty final evaluation. This prudent approach is especially helpful for those who understand that they are engaged in a living process. Still, it may make others uncomfortable as they proceed with caution and with patience. None should doubt, however, the Church's desire to meet this challenge, a challenge embraced by the Fathers of the Second Vatican Council.[6]

We would like to express our profound gratitude to all of those clergy, religious, pastoral ministers, liturgical scholars, and devoted faithful who directly contributed to this statement in ways that clearly demonstrate their generous service to the Church; their esteem of our African American heritage; their pursuit of scholarship and excellence; and their commitment to the African American Catholic community, which gratefully and humbly accepts their affection, support, and assistance. We are also grateful to all those who made a critique of the drafts, offered suggestions, and reviewed our work. We pray that they will find satisfaction in our common effort.

Most Reverend Wilton D. Gregory, SLD
Auxiliary Bishop of Chicago
Chairman, Bishops' Committee on the Liturgy

Liturgy and
Symbolic Reality

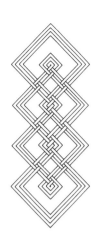

Liturgy and Symbolic Reality

You awake us to delight in your praise, for you have made us for yourself, and our heart is restless until it rests in you.[1]

A. An Examination of Ritual

1. Public worship, rooted in humanity's response to God's self-revelation, is a rich and complex reality. Although every people attempts to convey its awareness of absolute mystery, dread, awe, wonder, and love in its experience of the holy, ultimately, there are no adequate words for this ineffable mystery. The experience nonetheless is real, and it leads to a profound sense of total dependence, of utter creaturehood in the presence of the Creator. This experience of the absolute majesty of God, the One who dwells in unapproachable light, who is the source of life and goodness, is tempered by the equally powerful sense of the fascinating nearness and familiarity of God, who created all things and fills them with every blessing.[2]

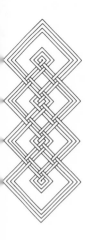

For without God all of our efforts turn to ashes and our sunrises into darkest nights. Without God, life is a meaningless drama with the decisive scenes missing. But with God we are able to rise from the fatigue of despair to the buoyancy of hope. With God we are able to rise from the midnight of desperation to the daybreak of joy. Saint Augustine was right—we were made for God and we will be restless until we find rest in God.[3]

This is uniquely true in the Christian tradition, because in Jesus Christ the mystery of the divine and of the human are both made manifest.[4] For by his dying and rising, "Jesus revealed the human face of God and transformed the face of humanity."[5] He is, as Saint Paul says, an unshakable "Yes" both to God and to us (see 2 Cor 1:18-22).

2.   Liturgy celebrates and evokes the divine reality that is at once remote and intimate, transcendent and immanent, beyond our reach and ever present. As a result, liturgy has an undeniable density and complexity even when worshipers and religious leaders themselves do not advert to it.[6] Liturgy evokes a world that is at once shared with others and is at the same time beyond ordinary life. To borrow the words of Howard Thurman, liturgy "bathes one's whole being with something more wonderful than words can ever tell."[7]

B. Symbols

3.   Because liturgy is concerned with realities of faith that go beyond immediate experience, it celebrates mystery by means of symbols and signs.[8] Liturgical activity, therefore, is not principally concerned about directly producing effects in the world as it is, except insofar as they relate to the coming of God's reign. Thus, in ritual activity, the faithful do not eat and drink only to feed their bodies. They do not sing only to make music. They do not speak only to teach and to learn. They do not pray only to restore psychic equilibrium. By using space, time, action, and speech in a new way, worship turns the attention of the assembly toward realities that would otherwise go unattended.[9] Worship lifts people up and moves them into the soul-stirring, the awe-inspiring, the transcendent, and the inciting[10] so that, ultimately, they may worship in spirit and truth (cf. Jn 4:24), so that they may not honor Christ in worship clothed in silk vestments, only to pass him by unclothed and frozen outside.[11]

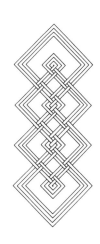

4.   Since liturgy is possible only by reason of humanity's intrinsic symbol-making genius, and because of the depth and complexity of both humanity and its symbols, it is possible for our symbols to be misused and misunderstood in the Sunday liturgy.

5.   First, one cannot arbitrarily make or establish symbols. Symbols are not merely things. Certain realities become symbolic in particular circumstances and only in relation to a human community. In and of themselves bread, wine, water, oil, fire, incense, a cross, a fish, a white robe, an organ melody, a purple cloth, a paragraph from Scripture may not be symbolic. They become symbolic because of their resonating with the members of a given historical, cultural, ethnic, and racial community. They can assume levels of meaning that make sense of birth, life, and death—by means of tradition, community, and grace.[12]

6.   Second, symbols are not to be confused with signs. Signs have conventional meanings established by the community. The purpose of a sign is clear and unambiguous (e.g., a red light means stop, and only stop; a green light means go, and only go). They are signs. There is no ambiguity. This is not the case with symbols. Symbols are necessarily ambiguous, that is, they evoke multiple meanings and associations. Water, for example, is a primal symbol. For different people, in different circumstances, a body of water may evoke very diverse symbolic associations: coolness, calm, life, storm, danger, drowning, flood, death. For this reason, symbols cannot be strictly controlled in an effort to manage and predict exactly what associations and feelings people will have in their presence.[13]

7.   This is why people can participate in the same celebration of the Eucharist on Sunday and find different meanings in the Scriptures proclaimed, the hymns sung, the preparation of the gifts, the eucharistic prayer, the sign of peace, the sharing in the Body and Blood of the Lord. This is also why people of different ethnic and cultural backgrounds may have different subjective responses to the same objective symbolic activity.

8.   Third, it is inadequate to think of symbols primarily as bearers of knowledge or information. While there is a catechetical and instructional dimension to the liturgy, the Eucharist is not the same as a religion class. It is a serious mistake to judge the impact of symbols by what people explicity un-

derstand by them, and even worse by what they can put into words. Moved by symbols, the faithful often know and understand far more than they can say.

9.   The Second Vatican Council and the postconciliar liturgical instructions of the Church enriched the symbols of the liturgy by restoring to the rites much of their original simplicity and beauty. This restoration emphasized the importance of the participation of the assembly, revised all existing rites, expanded the use of Scripture, and encouraged a greater degree of cultural diversity. As a result, the liturgy should be more understandable to the assembly and should invite the participation of all. Moreover, these enriched symbols have an authentic driving force even when they seem beyond comprehension. A person may be particularly moved by the singing of a certain hymn, by an element in one of the rites of Christian initiation, by the ritualized actions of vested ministers, or by the rich ceremonies of Holy Week without fully understanding them in the cognitive sense. Were they asked, "What do these symbols mean?" they might respond, "I don't know. I didn't even know they were symbols!" This would not imply that they have not experienced meaning in their symbolic activity. They have, for symbols are truly multidimensional phenomena.

10.   Again, if people are asked why they are deeply moved by the recitation of a poem by Langston Hughes, a sermon preached by Martin Luther King, Jr., jazz played by Mary Lou Williams, music scored by Lionel Hampton, the blues sung by Ray Charles, an aria performed by Marian Anderson, or a ballet choreographed by Alvin Ailey, they might be able to discourse on aesthetic theory, but they might not be able to say why the work moves them so. The interplay between symbol and person is far more than that of cause and effect. Symbols draw upon the accumulated wisdom and heritage of a people. They combine concepts and values, while appealing to memory and imagination. They derive much of their power through association with the collective experience and history of a people. Perhaps one of the reasons why some Catholic assemblies do not experience the full depth of their liturgical prayer is that the seeming ordinariness of their lives and daily work in some way separates them from poetic, artistic, and symbolic language. Such a difficulty might suggest a greater catechesis *through* and *for* the liturgy by "attending to what we and others actually experience in liturgy; reflecting on what our experience and that of others means; applying what we have learned to future liturgies."[14]

**Liturgy and the
Christ Event**

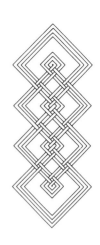

 **iturgy and the Christ Event**

A. Who and What Liturgy Celebrates

11.   Liturgy celebrates the landscapes of human experience: happiness, sadness, renewal, and grief. Liturgy provides rites of passage in human life: birth, maturity, vocation, commitment, old age, death. Liturgy also celebrates the universal human need for communion, healing, and reconciliation. Christian liturgy embraces all these and far more by celebrating the new meaning that the life, death, and resurrection of Jesus Christ give to the lives of all people. In the liturgy, the Church proclaims the paschal mystery, the paradigmatic event that transforms the past, the present, and the future. In faith, and in fact, the liturgy is the memorial that joins the worshipers to the past experience of the mystery of Christ that radically changed the lives of his followers and altered the history of the world. It is this memorial that directs worshipers into the future, the "not-yet" of Christ's coming in glory.[15]

12.   In the liturgy, Christ speaks to each person and each community in their lived conditions. Saint Augustine reminds

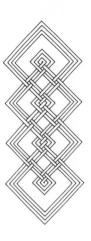

us: "He [Christ] has ascended without leaving us. While in heaven he is also with us, and while on earth we are also with him."[16] In this manner, people are able to unite the drama of their own sufferings with the paschal mystery of the Lord. The liturgy encourages the people of God, nourished by Christ's Body and Blood and filled with his Holy Spirit,[17] to approach the future with hope and trust. Even though this future is unknown, faith guarantees that Christ will be there. This confident hope embraces everyone's personal history as well as the future of the world. Believers realize that their faith in Christ makes them conscious that they must do everything they can to overcome personal problems and world discord, to be a living sacrifice of praise.[18] The liturgy also reminds them that when they have done all they can, they should not despair, because Christ is still with them. Events and experiences that seem random and confusing to them may be part of a larger, providential design beyond their complete understanding. It is this Christ event that all Catholics celebrate in the liturgy. It is this Christ event without which we cannot go on living.[19] It is this Christ event that is the hinge event of history, whose meaning surpasses the limits of time and locality.

B. The Encounter with Christ

13.   In whatever locality he preached, Jesus announced that the reign of God was at hand (see Mk 1:15). Wherever he traveled, Jesus turned people's hearts to God (see Lk 18:42-43). Whenever he proclaimed the Good News, Jesus showed the way to God's prodigal love and mercy (see Lk 15:11-32). Whoever followed him experienced in Jesus the very mystery of God. In him, their longings for a coming High Priest, Prophet, King, Suffering Servant, Savior, and Messiah were all fulfilled. He was the Christ, the Son of the living God (see Mt 16:13-23). The encounter with Christ changed their lives completely (see Lk 8:1-3). They could never forget the sacred meal that he left them (see 1 Cor 11:23-26), the meal that kept the memory of the Passover of the Lord but which they would now eat in memory of the Lord's dying and rising "until he comes" (see 1 Cor 11:26).[20] They experienced the devastation of his death (see Mt 27:45-66) and the joyous reality of his resurrection (see Jn 20:1-21,25). These experiences drew them deeper into the mystery of God. They preserved and passed onto others the meaning and truth of their encounter with Christ by means of oral and written accounts, by creeds, and most important, by liturgical symbols and rites

(see Acts 2:42). These symbols and rites have been continually adapted, depending upon the varying cultures encountered. The goal of the adaptations has always been to intensify the experience of the mystery of Christ and God's saving power for all peoples—even to the very ends of the earth (see Mt 28:16-20).

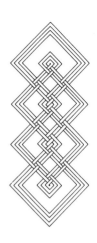

Liturgy and Culture

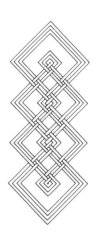

iturgy and Culture

A. The Encounter with Christ Continued Cultural Adaptation of the Liturgy throughout History

14.   From the beginning, in order to recall and relive the experience of Christ in their midst, the Church, at Jesus' command and under the guidance of the Holy Spirit, engaged and transformed many Jewish rituals, symbols, gestures, and customs beloved by Jesus and his original disciples.

15.   In this early and fertile Jewish period (c. 33 to c. 100), the Church harvested not only many followers but also words and phrases such as: *alleluia*; *amen*; "holy, holy, holy"; "it is right and just to give thanks and praise"; and "let us pray." It likewise gave a Christian meaning to the essential structure of the Eucharistic Prayer, intercessory prayer, and the liturgy of the word; baptismal rites, devotion to the saints, and laying on of hands; and designation of Sunday as the weekly day of worship.[21]

16.   As the Church grew, it continued its mission to the very ends of the earth. It encountered and labored among both the

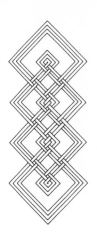

Hellenistic and Roman worlds. From this period (c. 100 and c. 321), the Church acquired the wisdom of Justin Martyr, Clement of Alexandria, Tertullian, Hippolytus and other learned doctors; words and phrases such as: *acclamation; advent; agape; anamnesis; canon; epiclesis; epiphany; eucharist; eulogy; Lord, have mercy; mystery;* and *preface;* the concepts of formulary prayer, sacrament, and silence; the rites of anointing, exorcism; the Church calendar;[22] and the *domus ecclesiae* (house of the Church), which was complete with an atrium where the assembly gathered, a large tank of water where the initiates could be baptized, and a table where the leader presided—all of which became the model space for assembly's worship.[23]

17.   With the peace established between Constantine and the Church in 313 by the Edict of Milan, the Church gained not only official recognition but also the new and free ideas of those such as Cyril of Jerusalem, Ambrose of Milan, John Chrysostom, and Augustine of Hippo; the concepts of mystagogy and of facing the East during prayer—prayer that was prayed through Christ, with Christ, and in Christ;[24] the continuing development of the Roman and Oriental Rites, baptismal candles, the washing of feet at baptism, and white baptismal garments; imperial court ceremonials; high esteem for the bishop and his office; liturgical vesture and ornaments, especially the pallium and ring; kissing the altar; and the establishment of the solemnity of Christmas—a prime example of cultural adaptation.[25]

18.   As the Church continued to develop, it heralded the Good News of the Christ-event to countless others. In the process of this proclamation, the Church became incarnate in new and varying cultures. During the Franco–Germanic period (c. 590 to c. 1073), the Church renewed its liturgical life and added to it the families of sacramentaries attributed to Leo the Great, Gelasius, and Gregory the Great; the lyrics of the "Veni Creator" and "Victimae Paschali"; devotion to the saints, liturgical drama, and verbal flourishes in prayer; the procession with palms on Palm Sunday, footwashing on Holy Thursday, the veneration of the cross on Good Friday; the blessing of the new fire, the greeting of the Light of Christ, the singing of the "Exultet," the blessing of the baptismal water at the Easter Vigil; Romanesque churches and their rites of dedication.[26] Simultaneously, from the East the Church reaped the bounty of the greatness of Cyril and Methodius in their adapting the Byzantine liturgy to the culture and language of the Slavic peoples.[27] All this activity served as pow-

erful testimony to Saint Peter's early admonition: "In truth, I see that God shows no partiality. Rather, in every nation whoever fears him and acts uprightly is acceptable to him" (Acts 10:34-35).[28]

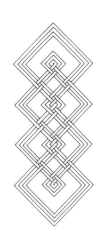

19. With the passage of time, the Church continued to grow even further and farther it reached the very limits of the known world. Having converged with the world's manifold cultures and having adapted worthily to them, the Church regrettably, as Anscar Chupungco has stated, entered upon a period of "luxuriant growth in which the liturgy was both reinterpreted and misinterpreted."[29] The first chill in the mid-winter of the Church's liturgical adaptation was felt in the political policies of Saint Pope Gregory VII (c. 1021-1085); the unification of the Western liturgies through the agency of mendicant preachers; elaborate liturgical plays, with actors supplanting the solemn liturgical actions of the assembly; the multiplication of Masses, with the attendant diminution of the liturgical ministries coupled with an exaggerated piety toward the Eucharist apart from the eucharistic action and the reception of Holy Communion; and all this to the increased accompaniment of sacring-bells and the song of paid chantry clerks.[30] Of this age, Walter Howard Frere writes:

> Equally unfortunate was the effect on persons. The Mass-priest became dominant. Now, so long as he had a serving boy, he could dispense with deacon and other ministers; he could supersede the congregation also. With the disappearance of the sense of sacrifice there disappeared also not only the layman's communion but also the sense of his lay-priesthood. The ideal layman was the boy who would serve the priest's Mass. Drill superseded worship and the Mass was commercialized. The hour of Low Mass arrived; and the hour of revulsion drew on.[31]

20. Because of the aforementioned factors, and out of the rapid expansion and sometimes unregulated practices of the Middle Ages, there arose a call for strict uniformity. A heightened rubrical approach followed the Council of Trent, whose principal aim was to curb abuses and institute reforms, not to introduce new adaptations. With the reform of the Roman Missal by Saint Pius V in 1570 and the establishment of the Sacred Congregation of Rites by Sixtus V in 1588, the centralizing effort of Trent was realized, free development of the liturgy in local churches was greatly curtailed, and the cultural accommodation of liturgy came to a virtual standstill.[32] One need only examine the Chinese Rites controversy to see how

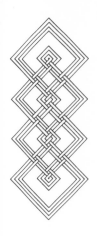

creative and daring adaptations of the faith and its practices to the Chinese Confucian culture of the sixteenth and seventeenth centuries came into direct conflict with the Church's desire for unification.[33] Liturgical creativity took avenues other than the Mass: devotion to the Blessed Sacrament, which gave rise to the use of tabernacles, sanctuary lights, elevations, exposition, and benediction.[34]

21.   In reaction to this period of strict uniformity and its consequent alienation of the assembly came the Age of the Baroque with its "flair for festivity, external manifestations of grandeur and triumphalism, especially through pilgrimages and processions, and sensuousness in artistic expression and pious devotions."[35]

22.   In time, some protested the inflexibility of the state of the liturgical life of the post-Tridentine Church as well as the externalism of the Baroque. With this protest developed the advent of Romanticism and its subsequent stress on history. The Church began to reexamine the origins and meaning of liturgical gestures, vestments, vessels, rites, and feasts.

23.   From the nineteenth century onward came renowned liturgists such as Prosper Gueranger, Virgil Michel, Odo Casel, Pius Parsch, Lambert Beauduin, and Romano Guardini; and the great liturgical centers at Solesmes, Beuron, Maredsous, Maria Laach, and Malines.[36] These scholars and outstanding centers of renewed liturgical life provided the foundation of the Liturgical Movement of the early 1900s, which culminated in Pius XII's encyclical on the sacred liturgy, *Mediator Dei*, in 1947; the reformation of the Holy Week Rites in 1955; and finally, the magna carta of contemporary liturgical renewal, the *Constitution on the Liturgy* of the Second Vatican Council, which was promulgated by Paul VI on December 4, 1963.[37]

B. Cultural Adaptation and the Second Vatican Council

24.   Throughout much of its history, the Church was firmly committed to cultural adaptation in public worship for the good of the people of God. The same is true of the Church today. The *Constitution on the Liturgy*, the principal guide for the pastoral adaptation of the liturgy, reminds us of the communal and unifying nature of the liturgy:

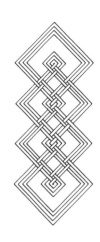

Liturgical services are not private functions, but are celebrations belonging to the Church, which is the "sacrament of unity," namely, the holy people united and ordered under their bishops.[38]

Yet, recognizing the diversity of Christian communities, the missionary nature of the Church, and the exigencies of evangelization, the Church teaches that liturgical rites may be adapted to the temperaments and traditions of different ethnic, language, cultural, and racial groups. With due respect for the common good and unity of faith, the Church does not wish to impart a rigid uniformity upon liturgical expression. Rather, when local customs are free of superstition and error, they may be admitted into the liturgy "provided they are in keeping with the true and authentic spirit of the liturgy."[39]

25. While clearly calling for the safeguarding of the substantial unity of the Roman Rite, the Church insists that there be legitimate variations and adaptations to different groups, regions, and peoples in drawing up rites, determining rubrics, and revising liturgical books. This is particularly important in areas where the Church is still very young or very small.[40] Therefore, within the limits specified by the liturgical books themselves, specific adaptations may be made in the style of celebrating the sacraments, sacramentals, processions, liturgical language, music, and art by competent territorial ecclesiastical authority.[41]

26. Because the bishops of the Second Vatican Council, assembled from all over the world, were quite aware of the racial, cultural, and spiritual differences of the people of their local churches and of the millions of people yet to hear or respond to the gospel of Christ, they provided for "even more radical adaptations." Such adaptations are always to be guided by the following considerations:

a) The competent, territorial ecclesiastical authority mentioned in art. 22, par. 2, must, in this matter, carefully, and prudently weigh what elements from the traditions and culture of individual peoples may be appropriately admitted into divine worship. They are to propose to the Apostolic See adaptations considered useful or necessary that will be introduced with its consent.

b) To ensure that adaptations are made with all the circumspection they demand, the Apostolic See will grant power to

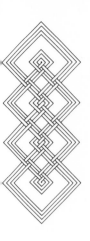

this same territorial ecclesiastical authority to permit and to direct, as the case requires, the necessary preliminary experiments within certain groups suited for the purpose and for a fixed time.

c) Because liturgical laws often involve special difficulties with respect to adaptation, particularly in mission lands,[42] experts in these matters must be employed to formulate them.[43]

27. The Church further recognized that there is a necessary connection between liturgical adaptations and ongoing catechesis. The *Constitution on the Liturgy* expressed well the Church's desire to ensure that no one in the Church feel estranged or alienated, but that those who are invited to the feast be able to participate fully:

> The Church, therefore, earnestly desires that Christ's faithful, when present at this mystery of faith, should not be there as strangers or silent spectators; on the contrary, through a good understanding of the rites and prayers they should take part in the sacred service conscious of what they are doing, with devotion and full involvement. They should be instructed by God's word and be nourished at the table of the Lord's body; they should give thanks to God; by offering the immaculate Victim, not only through the hands of the priest, but also with him, they should learn to offer themselves as well; through Christ the Mediator, they should be formed day by day into an ever more perfect unity with God and with each other, so that finally God may be all in all.[44]

28. In its continuing implementation of the reforms initiated by the Second Vatican Council, the Church has spoken still further on the direct connection between liturgical adaptation and evangelization:

> In the work of evangelization the liturgy clearly holds a place of primary importance: it stands as a high point at which the preached mystery of salvation becomes actual; pastorally it offers to evangelization privileged occasions and a sound and effective formation. . . . The intimate union between evangelization and liturgy also gives rise to the duty of renewing the liturgical celebration; this will unfailingly have a strong impact on the life of the Church.[45]

Liturgical Adaptation in
the African American
Community

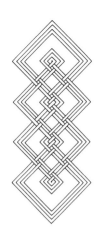

 **iturgical Adaptation in the African American Community**

A. The Call

29.   The aforementioned summary statements about liturgical uniformity, diversity, catechesis, and evangelization should make it clear that the Church is sincerely and fundamentally committed to translating its liturgical rites to the many voices of various people, creating, it is hoped, one song of praise.

30.   Nowhere is this commitment more profoundly expressed than in Paul VI's speech to the young churches in Africa:

The expression, that is, the language and mode of manifesting this one faith, may be manifold; hence, it may be original, suited to the tongue, the style, the character, the genius and the culture of the one who professes this one faith. From this point of view, a certain pluralism is not only legitimate, but desirable. An adaptation of the Christian life in the fields of pastoral, ritual, didactic, and spir-

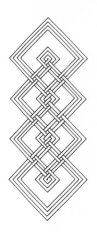

itual activities is not only possible, it is even favored by the Church. The liturgical renewal is a living example of this. And in this sense you may, and you must, have an African Christianity. Indeed you possess human values and characteristic forms of culture which rise up to perfection such as to find in Christianity and for Christianity a true superior fullness and prove to be capable of a richness of expression all its own, and genuinely African. . . . You will be capable of bringing to the Catholic Church the precious and original contribution of "Blackness" which she particularly needs in this historic hour.[46]

31.   What Paul VI asked of Africans for the universal Church, the Church in the United States asks of its African American daughters and sons—the gift of "Blackness," a gift so intensely expressive and so alive that it comes from the very depths of the Black soul, a gift not just to improve the work of evangelization but to further the very Catholic nature that is the Church's.[47]

32.   The Catholic Church indeed welcomes the genius and talents of African Americans. Witness but a few of the many recent signs of growth and vitality of the Church in that community:

- *Discrimination and Christian Conscience* (1958); *On Racial Harmony* (1963); *Statement on the National Race Crisis* (1968); *Brothers and Sisters to Us* (1979)[48]—challenging statements and pastoral letters of the National Conference of Catholic Bishops condemning the sin of racism and calling for a commitment to eradicate it;

- the ordination of our African American brothers to the episcopacy and the issuing of *What We Have Seen and Heard*,[49] their illustrative pastoral letter on the nature of evangelization in the African American community;

- the clear inclusion of African American leaders at all levels of church government;

- the establishment of diocesan offices of ministry to the African American community;

- the creation of a Secretariat for Black Catholics at the National Conference of Catholic Bishops;

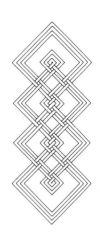

- the Sixth National Black Catholic Congress, its subsequent compelling Pastoral Plan, and its continuing conferences and workshops to assist those who minister in the African American community;

- the introduction and publication of *Lead Me, Guide Me* (GIA Publications, Inc., 1987), the first African American Catholic hymnal, and *In Spirit and Truth: Black Catholic Reflections on the Order of Mass* (USCC, 1987);

- the secure foundation of quality liturgical programs throughout the United States for African Americans;

- a host of diocesan-wide revivals and festive celebrations commemorating Dr. Martin Luther King, Jr. and Black History Month;

- the ever-increasing creation of African American choirs to employ the wide range of the African American musical heritage; and

- John Paul II's spirited meeting with representatives of the African American Catholic community in New Orleans during his 1987 pastoral visit to the United States, where he stated:

> While remaining faithful to her doctrine and discipline, the Church esteems and honors all cultures; she respects them in all her evangelizing efforts among the various peoples. At the first Pentecost, those present heard the apostles speaking in their own languages (cf. Acts 2:4ff). With the guidance of the Holy Spirit, we try in every age to bring the gospel convincingly and understandably to people of all races, languages, and cultures. It is important to realize that there is no black Church, no white Church, no American Church; but there is and must be, in the one Church of Jesus Christ, a home for blacks, whites, Americans, every culture and race. What I said on another occasion, I willingly repeat: "The Church is catholic . . . because she is able to present in every human context the revealed truth, preserved by her intact in its divine content, in such a way as to bring it into contact with the lofty thoughts and just expectations of every individual and every people" (*Slavorum Apostoli*, 18).

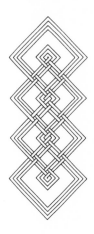

Dear brothers and sisters, your black cultural heritage enriches the Church and makes her witness of universality more complete. In a real way the Church needs you, just as much as you need the Church, for you are part of the Church and the Church is part of you. . . . [50]

33.   The Church's commitment to and call for liturgical adaptation are clear. The Church's commitment to and call for liturgical adaptation in the African American community are clear and unequivocal. Yet, the continuation of the task at hand is involved and complex.

B. The Early Years of the Church in the United States: A Dominance of Western Culture through Missionary Activity

34.   Sadly, many Americans, even a number of African American Catholics, perceive and experience the Catholic Church in the United States as an exclusively white European reality. This is due in part to the centuries-old Catholic tradition associated with countries like Italy, France, Spain, Germany, Poland, and Ireland and with the great missionaries of the Church who were noted for having brought the faith from these Christian countries to peoples of distant lands.

35.   In the United States, Catholicism was introduced primarily through the colonizing vigor of the Spanish, French, and English.[51]

36.   Inspired by the drive to announce the reign of God to Native Americans and European settlers, Franciscans, Dominicans, Jesuits, and Sulpicians evangelized Florida, the Southwest, Texas, California, Canada, the Great Lakes region, Maryland, Pennsylvania, and New York.

37.   During this Spanish, French, and English missionary activity, Catholicism was so intimately wed to the culture of the missionaries that, doubtless, many of them could not easily distinguish the Gospel that they preached from their own particular cultural expression of it. As a result, because of its links to Europe and its history, the Church in America, like most American institutions, tended to assume that European cultures were the only cultures and found it extremely difficult to imagine, much less value, cultures other than their own.

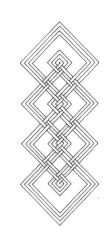

38. Happily, for the better part of this century, there has been a gradual change in the understanding of human experience and human perception, particularly by those who are expert observers and evaluators of cultures. There is a greater awareness that European cultures are not normative.

39. As long as Europe was recognized as the "center of gravity," many people perceived European cultures as the norm, as the only "real" cultures. In scholarly circles and in common parlance, these cultures came to be called "classical." They were viewed as a distillation of the great achievements of ancient Greek philosophy, Roman political systems, and Western European philosophy, art, music, architecture, and social values. And they were viewed as universal, providing the normative understanding of the human condition, the nature of religion, and the social order. For generations, these "classical" cultures held sway, and in some quarters they continue to hold sway even today as the only authentic expressions of culture. Consequently, the mores, customs, traditions, folkways, rituals, and symbols of people who are not European were rarely, if ever, considered expressions of culture, especially as these people were viewed as "primitive," "barbaric," and "uncivilized." Recent evidence for this can be found, for example, in the way Native, African, and Asian American peoples were portrayed in American film and television from the 1930s until the late 1960s and in the fact that the art and artifacts of Africa have only recently been deemed worthy of a place in American and European art museums.

C. Contemporary Understanding of Culture

40. Fortunately, contemporary understanding of culture is quite different. In the contemporary view, no one culture is normative, and all races and ethnic groups are to be taken seriously. Indeed, all peoples have customs, mores, artistic expressions, and traditions that constitute genuine culture. Furthermore, this contemporary view of culture has a historical perspective. It accepts and embraces diversity and pluralism in a manner that the "classical" cultures never could. European "classical" culture is accepted as one among many expressions of culture.

41. For centuries, the Church shaped and influenced European cultures in an intimate way, and, most assuredly, European cultures had an equal impact on the Church. The neces-

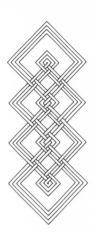

sary process of ridding what is obsolete in this "classical" view of culture and assimilating what is of value in the contemporary view of culture is painstakingly difficult. Nevertheless, it is just such a process that is essential in promoting liturgical adaptation in the African American community.

42.   The fact that the Church is renewing its recognition of and warmly embracing a plurality of cultures does not mean that it must abandon the rich liturgical and aesthetic traditions developed in Europe.[52] What must happen, and indeed what is already happening, is that the Church welcomes and strongly encourages the equally rich and diverse traditions of all peoples in every time and in every place.

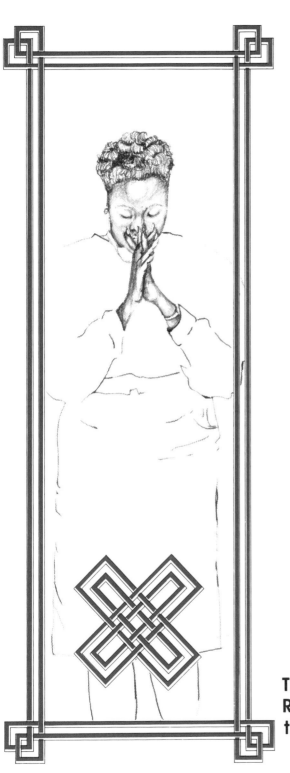

The African American Religious Experience in the United States

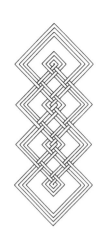

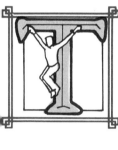# he African American Religious Experience in the United States

A. A Varied People

43.   Before all else, and in order better to understand Roman Catholic worship in the African American community, it must first be stated that the African American community is not monolithic. Even the term "African American" is not universally used. Many people prefer other descriptions, such as "Negro," "African," "Afro-American," "Black," or simply "people of color." Still others think of themselves only as human beings. Race, for them, is a secondary reality that merits neither discrimination nor special treatment.

44.   African Americans live, work, study, and recreate in a wide variety of social settings. There is indeed a great diversity in nations of origin, socioeconomic status, religious and political persuasions, historical backgrounds, and life-styles. Strictly speaking, African American enslavement was not the

universal experience of all "African" people in the United States. Yet, while slavery was not an experience common to all African Americans, racism, which has been part of the social fabric of America since its European colonization and which persists still today in many blatant and covert ways, was.

45. Some African Americans do not wish to be thought of as "African American Catholics." Rather, they simply regard themselves as Catholics. They may cherish the Gregorian *Missa Orbis Factor* or may relish singing traditional hymns and contemporary songs as much as their white counterparts. These traditional Black Catholics should not be treated as "odd, misinformed, or pitiable souls," but they must be respected, for all Catholics are indeed our brothers and sisters in the faith. They, along with many other Catholics, may need to be reminded that, some twenty-five years after the Second Vatican Council, reform and renewal of the liturgy are at the very heart of the Church's life and mission today. Others, unfortunately, may have to be persuaded to overcome in themselves any subtle form of self-hatred that is an unsightly fragment of years of sustained racism.

46. Despite this diversity, the vast majority of African American Catholics, both convert and "cradle Catholic," upper middle-class and poor, would attest with their African American brothers in the episcopacy that

> There is a richness in our Black experience that we must share with the entire people of God. These are gifts that are part of an African past. For we have heard with Black ears and have seen with Black eyes, and we have understood with an African heart. We thank God for the gifts of our Catholic faith, and we give thanks for the gifts of our Blackness. In all humility we turn to the whole Church that it might share our gifts so that "our joy may be complete."
>
> To be Catholic is to be universal. To be universal is not to be uniform. It does mean, however, that the gifts of individuals and of particular groups become the common heritage shared by all. Just as we lay claim to the gifts of Blackness, so we share these gifts within the Black community at large and within the Church. This will be our part in the building up of the whole Church. This will also be our way of enriching ourselves. "For it is in giving that we receive." Finally, it is our way to witness to

our brothers and sisters within the Black community that the Catholic Church is both one and also home to us all.[53]

B. The Broader Context

47.   African American religious experience is shaped by African factors as well as by those on these shores. To begin with, several key concepts should be noted:

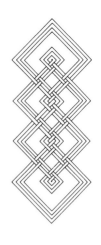

- that religion is an all-pervasive reality for African peoples;[54]

- that a sense of the holy encompasses the whole mystery of life, beginning before birth and continuing after death;[55]

- that for most Africans, to live is to participate in a religious drama;[56] and

- that African people see themselves as totally immersed in a sacred cosmos.[57]

This was the religious cultural matrix of many African Americans who accepted Christianity in this country.

48.   Although current evidence seems to suggest that those Africans who were enslaved here were not brought from African territories where Christianity may have existed, we must nevertheless remember that Christianity was indeed no stranger to African cultures. Actually, Christianity had been well established in much of North Africa, parts of the Sudan, Egypt, and Ethiopia. This was a dynamic Christianity, one that produced great scholars and theologians such as Clement of Alexandria, Tertullian, Origen, Cyprian of Carthage, Augustine of Hippo, and Pope Gelasius. Ethiopia was evangelized in the fourth century by Saint Frumentius, whom Saint Athanasius selected to be bishop. In the sixth century, the Emperor Justinian and the Empress Theodora, respectively, sent two groups of missionaries to evangelize Nubia (modern-day Sudan). Until Islamic armies conquered the area in the seventh century, many North Africans made significant contributions to the Church. The Moslem conquest reduced the Church in North Africa to a mere remnant, and by the year 1000 much of North Africa's Church was extinct.

49.   Once in the United States, enslaved Africans had some contact with the Catholic Church in those areas where Catho-

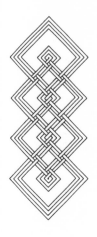

lics were numerous. In other areas where the slave holders were Protestant, they had little, if any, initial contact with the Catholic Church. These enslaved people responded most favorably, however, to the evangelizing efforts of Methodist and Baptist preachers. The fact that these preachers were willing to allow the enslaved to express freely the religious feelings of their hearts contributed greatly to the growth of the Protestant churches among Africans in the United States. Protestant revivals,[58] camp meetings, and the growth of the "secret church," that is, the church under the trees, the church in chains, the church in the fields—the church not doctrinally, institutionally, nor juridically denominational; that church of the slave quarters and family gatherings, where the spirituals were born, sung, danced, prayed, shouted, sermonized; where the sin-sick soul was healed—all gave the enslaved Africans hope of at least a spiritual escape from their oppression.

C. The U.S. Religious Experience in Detail

50.   The experience of the African American religious origins here in the United States bears a deeper scrutiny. The enslaved African women and men brought with them to this continent a concept of the Supreme Being, who was deeply and continually involved in the practical affairs of their daily lives, but in a different way than the Christian God.[59]

> For Africans believed in a God who was not only omnipresent, omniscient, omnipotent, and eternal, they believed in a God, who as Supreme Being, had a radical moral relationship with humanity. This Being was approachable through many intermediaries, especially nature—all symbolic representatives of the living, pulsating environment in which humans subsist and through which we are related to the spirits of natural things and the ancestors, but preeminently with the Supreme Being, the God who is above all gods and who is known as Creator, Judge, and Redeemer.[60]

This God and their belief in this God helped them to survive.

Scripture

51.   When the enslaved began to learn Bible stories, beginning with Adam and Eve and continuing through to the ministry of Jesus; Jesus' suffering, death, and resurrection; and

the Day of Judgment,[61] they developed a unique theological vision that spoke directly to their plight. They concluded that the God of the Bible was the same universal guide and ruler of the religion of their forebears:

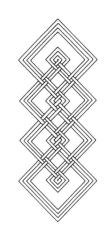

> God is a God.
> God don't never change!
> God is a God.
> An' He always will be God.
> (Spiritual: "God Is A God")[62]

This God cared for and rewarded all people who were good and punished all who were wicked. This God was not partial to the enslaved or the free; men or women; black or white; brown, yellow, or red; for there would be "plenty good room in my Father's Kingdom" (Spiritual: "Plenty Good Room").[63]

52. Though uprooted and far from home, the enslaved now found a basic orientation and harmony in the scriptural world. These enslaved people from Africa, now baptized, knew that the God of the Bible was a God of liberation, a God who set captives free, who sent Moses "to tell ole Pharaoh to let my people go" (Spiritual: "Go Down, Moses").[64] They understood that this God did not accept slavery any more than sin. And they decided that, if the God of Hebrew children would work to free them and give them a homeland, and if the God of Jesus Christ so loved the world that the only-begotten Son was given to the world to be its Savior, then this same God must love them too. This God would not leave them in bondage under the taskmaster's whip forever. They would indeed be "free at last. Thank God Almighty we're free at last!" (Spiritual: "Free At Last").[65]

53. Those few enslaved who were able to read were particularly ignited by the Scriptures and often went from camp to camp sharing the encouraging word of what God had done and what God could indeed still do.

54. In continuing to tell the Bible's story to each other again and again, the slaves came to recognize more powerfully their own story in the Bible. They were a scattered people of many tribal origins, all of whom involuntarily had been enslaved for the service of another nation. They had cried out to the God of their ancestors for deliverance, and they had been answered by a God they did not at first know. They soon learned that this God was the God of their ancestors, and

entering their lives, this God constituted them as a beloved people, a light to the nations (see Is 42:6).

55.   These enslaved Africans discovered their own story in the story of Jesus as well, for he identified with those who were poor, blind, and suffering. Like so many of them, Jesus had been born into an oppressed class, suffered real pain, carried a real cross, died a real human death. But he had overcome it all for their sake. And in his resurrection, Jesus showed himself their Lord and Savior, guaranteeing deliverance to his friends, promising to come again when "the Lord shall bear my spirit home."[66]

56.   Enslaved African people in America accepted Christianity because it explained their unique situation: God saw a suffering people; Jesus took up their burden, and he had changed the world, changed the history of the African American slave, lifting it and pointing it toward divine expectations: the freedom of the children of God (see Rom 8:21).

The Invisible Institution

57.   This unique Christian vision of the enslaved African Americans resulted in a religion that strengthened them in times of great adversity.[67] This same vision gave birth to the "Black church"—the "invisible institution"[68]—when, out of fear of African American uprisings, religious services by the enslaved were forbidden unless overseen by whites. This church "became the religion of double blackness, carried on in the shadows and under cover of the night, always in danger of interruption and punishment so severe that it might even mean death."[69] Like any other highly developed religion, the "invisible institution," whose vestiges are visible even today, had its sacred space, sacred time, and sacred action.[70]

58.   Its sacred space was the woods in the evening, groupings around camp fires, secret gatherings in a cabin, stealing away under trees, standing in an open field. These places were called "hush-harbors," places where softly spoken words and sacred chants were secretly, yet boldly uttered.

59.   Its sacred time was a gentle combination of God's time and their own life cycle. It was a time in which one, wearing a white robe, could be fully immersed in the saving waters of baptism and enfolded in the community's love. It was a time where two, who could be sold separately, were made one in the midst of a joyous community. It was a time when one

could die, but not be forgotten, ever living in the hearts and minds of a remembering community.

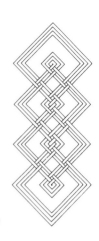

60. Its sacred action was prayer, preaching, and conversion supported by gesture and sacred song. The Scripture was proclaimed and broken open by one who was "acquainted with the source of sacred knowledge."[71] The preacher's ability to dramatize and apply the sacred texts to the assembly's lives in burning oratory, and sometimes solemnly chanted sermons, had to be unparalleled. It had to lead people to "conversion," a radical change of heart ending in a sense of cleanliness, certainty, and reintegration—the three things every enslaved person was denied in life.[72] The minister's ability to lift up the assembly by eloquent, poetic prayer, large gestures, and spirited song encouraged the assembly to do the same.

Spirituals

61. Recalling the melodies of Mother Africa; using the hymnody of a new land; recalling the stories from the Bible; and using clapping, moaning, shouting, waving hands, and dance, this community sang songs of life and death, suffering and sorrow, love and judgment, grace and hope, justice and mercy. They sang ardently and lovingly, often hoping against hope. And in singing these "spirituals," they expressed all manner of things:[73]

- their anguish in slavery ("I've Been Buked And I've Been Scorned");[74]

- their trust in God's mighty arm ("Didn't My Lord Deliver Daniel?");[75]

- their belief in God's care ("Nobody Knows The Trouble I See");[76]

- their identification with Jesus' suffering, a suffering like their own ("Were You There When They Crucified My Lord?");[77]

- their belief in the resurrection ("Soon-a Will Be Done");[78]

- their desire for freedom ("O Freedom");[79]

- their assurance of certain freedom now sung in "double coded" songs ("Steal Away");[80] and

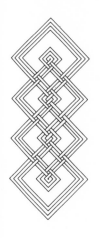

- their need for constant conversion and prayer ("Wade In The Water"; "Standin' In The Need Of Prayer").[81]

62. What must be noted here is that the Scriptures cited in these "spirituals" were not from the Douai–Rheims translation of the Bible, but from the King James translation. This is yet another one of the many clear reminders to us Roman Catholics that when the "Black church" was developed, most of the enslaved knew almost nothing about the Catholic Church.

Efforts at Evangelization

63. Though it is true that in the British colonies, during the seventeenth and eighteenth centuries, Roman Catholics were numerically and culturally an insignificant minority—most being found only in Maryland, in parts of Pennsylvania, and, by the beginning of the nineteenth century, in Kentucky and Louisiana—the Catholic Church, except in some isolated instances, was not at all aggressive in the evangelization of the Africans in America or in supporting the Abolitionist Movement to end slavery. As a result, the Church failed to seize the initiative in the evangelizing and converting of the African American population. This failure was due in great part to the acceptance of slavery as an institution by many of the Christian faithful and clergy. Tragically, there seems to have been no Saint Peter Claver or Bishop Bartolomé de las Casas to cry out in the wilderness of the United States.

64. Furthermore, there is one sad fact we can neither excuse nor ignore: the clergy and people of the Church in America did very little to evangelize African Americans; to expose them to the rich graces and strengths of Catholic life, tradition, and worship; or to lighten the weight of their suffering.

65. What efforts were made to evangelize African Americans began in earnest with the advent of Mary Elizabeth Lange and the Oblate Sisters of Providence in 1828, in Baltimore; Henriette Delille and the Sisters of the Holy Family in 1842, in New Orleans; the arrival of the Mill Hill Fathers (Josephites) from England in 1871, in Baltimore; and the founding of the Sisters of the Blessed Sacrament by Blessed Katharine Drexel two decades later in Philadelphia.[82]

66. In the 1920s and 1930s, African Americans migrated to the North in large numbers, hoping to escape the blatant rac-

ism in the South and searching for employment. The Jim Crow laws and the no less blatant segregation practiced in all northern cities resulted in "Negro parishes," similar to those already established in the South. Because there was no contact with "white parishes," there was little or limited shared experience of a common church life.

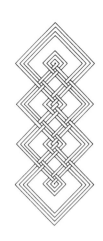

67.   Whenever a parish changed from serving white Americans to serving African Americans, the ordinary policy of most dioceses was to turn parish administration over to religious orders that were willing to take up the special ministry to African Americans. One dubious result of this segregated ministry was that certain religious orders attracted at least a few African American vocations, while most diocesan seminaries and communities of religious women attracted almost none.

68.   Unfortunately, because of this attitude toward African Americans, many in this century believe that the Church saw its work as little more than a burdensome endeavor to educate African Americans out of their "uncivilized and barbaric" traditions and into the European-American culture with which the Church seemed so fundamentally identified. That is why the Church's present efforts at evangelization and liturgical adaptation are all the more necessary and urgent, and yet all the more difficult to accomplish.

The African
American Church

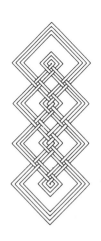

he African American Church

A. African Vestiges

69. The religious history of Africans and their descendants in this country is certainly a long and complex one. But, in spite of this troubled history, continuity with a rich African ritual has survived in the "Black church," if only in fragmentary ways, even to this very day. W. E. B. Du Bois, Albert J. Raboteau, and George Ofori-atta-Thomas inform us that ancient West African worship was marked by dramatic prayer, storytelling, teaching, song, poetic intensity, and by postures of praise, beauty of symbol, kinship, and healing. *Griots* (African storytellers) and others—persons who assisted the community in its encounter with the sacred—presided over these rituals, told the ancient story, and reminded the assembled who they were and whose they were.[83]

70. Robert C. Williams, Robert Farris Thompson, and Ulysses D. Jenkins tell us that the enslaved Africans, combining these ancient elements with a new understanding of the God

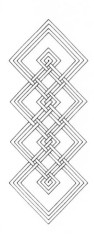

of Jesus, created a ritual process that was dramatic in character, influenced by the shout, and was the means by which conversion and God were experienced. They were thus enabled to follow a more or less orderly means of ritually seeking solutions to their problems—to "sing a song of the LORD in a foreign land" (Ps 137:4).[84]

B. The "Black Church" Today

71.　The vestiges of this transformed ritual process is present even now in many African American Protestant traditions. Today, we can still hear dramatic prayer:

> Dear God,
> 　　Enable us, we pray, to see your acts and to hear your voice amidst the rumbling and confusion of these earthquaking days. Equip us to seize the time that we may be vigilant in our freedom, committed in our callings, and just in our relations with all. *Amen.*[85]

72.　We can still hear the sermon "preached," employing Scripture, drama, sustained tones, intonation, rhythm, call-and-response, congregational identification, and a call to conversion:[86]

> As they went up to the temple to pray, a certain man— don't know the man's name, but the next few words tell us somewhat of his condition—a certain man that was lame from his mother's womb. When he said "a lame man," that made me feel sorry for him because it is a pitiful thing when a person has been useful and now has lost that usefulness.
> 　　But when I got to thinking about this man who was lame, and I remember the writer said that he was lame from his mother's womb, that made it all the more pitiful to me. For not only was he a lame man, but he had been lame all his life. And I can think of nothing more pitiful than a lame baby—one who was born into the world and whose parents have ever hoped some day he will be strong and healthy. I can see those parents watching him day in and day out, but he never had any use of his limbs. He grew old in age, but still lame.
> 　　I think it was last fall, or some time recently, a teenager was told that one of his legs would have to be amputated. He just hated the idea. "Here I am a teenager, where all of the other children my age are active in get-

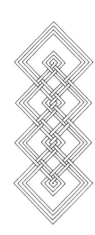

ting around, doing this and that; and conditions are such that I will have to lose one of my legs and be a cripple the rest of my life."

Well, it is a pitiful thing to see a teenager lame. But, here, this man had never been able to use his limbs, and had been lame from his mother's womb. This man had to be carried. You know we can understand this man's condition because he couldn't help himself. I know a lot of people in the church that are healthy and strong but still want to be carried . . . They had to carry this man and they brought him daily and laid him at a gate called Beautiful. Now they carried him daily, it means that he must have been receiving something that kept him coming back . . . Look at that man that was made by the hands of God. That man is lame and twisted, and had to be carried.

Well, when he saw Peter and John going into the temple, he got glad because, you know, he had begged so long until he could just look at a person as he approached and he could tell what kind of gift he was going to get. I can understand, somehow, how he felt. At one time I used to hop bells at a hotel. And, you know, after a few years I could look at a guest when he pulled up in front of the door and I could pretty well tell what kind of tip I was going to get. Oh, I could look at his bags, yes, I could . . . I could look at the way he was dressed and I could tell the type, the size of tip I was going to get.

Well, this man had been in this business so long until he could look and size up the kind of gift he was going to get. But this time he underestimated. Yes, he did! He knew he was looking for alms. He was looking for something that he could exchange at the supermarket. Oh, but Peter and John said, "Look on us." And every one of us who is representative of the Lord ought to be able to tell the world to "look on us . . ."[87]

73. We can still hear syncopated, heart-throbbing, feeling-thumping song, as varied as: "Do, Lord, Remember Me"[88] or Andre Crouch's "Soon And Very Soon"[89] or Leon Robert's "Holy, Holy, Holy."[90]

74. We can still hear kinship in warm, heartfelt fellowship:

On Sundays when services are to be held, the congregation gathers long before it is time to begin. As they drop in one or two at a time, there is much merriment. Each

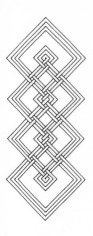

new arrival means a round of handshaking and earnest inquiry as to health.[91]

75. We can still hear partnership expressed:

Preacher: "Let the church say Amen!"
Church: "Amen. Praise the Lord. Hallelujah!"
or
"I hear you! Say so. Look out now. Go head!"

76. We can still feel the healing when persons "get the spirit" or "fall out" or are "slain in the Spirit." We see this healing acclaimed in witness, testimony, and spontaneous song as well.

**Toward an Authentic
African American
Catholic Worship**

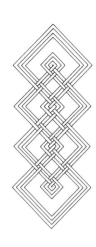

oward an Authentic
African American
Catholic Worship

A. Word and Sacrament

77.   First, when African American Catholics began to thirst
for African American cultural expressions in Roman Catholic
worship, they turned to those vestigial African traditions still
found in the Protestant churches. Initially, some Catholics
may have attempted to bring whole structures of African
American Protestant worship into Catholic liturgy exactly as
they experienced them. However, ecclesiological and credal
differences as well as theological and sociological analyses
suggest that most Baptist, Methodist, and Pentescostal practices simply cannot be, and nor should they be, translated
into Catholic liturgy. Specifically:

Though our liturgy is Catholic in that it is open to welcome the spiritual contributions of all peoples which are
consistent with our biblical faith and our historical conti-

nuity, it is also Catholic in that everything that is done in our worship clearly serves (and does not interrupt) this ritual action of Word and sacrament which has its own rhythm and movement, all built on the directions, rites, and forms of the Roman Catholic liturgy as they are approved and promulgated.[92]

African American Catholics "understand the clear distinction between the Roman Catholic Church as a sacramental-eucharistic community and Christian churches of the Protestant tradition as evangelical."[93]

B. Spirituality

78.   Second, African American Catholics turned to "Black theology" for inspiration. This theology, which is concerned with the desire of the African American community to know itself and to know God in the context of African American experience, history, and culture, is as old as the first sermon preached by enslaved Africans to their brothers and sisters huddled together in some plantation swamp, and as new as the reflections of James Cone, Major Jones, J. Deotis Roberts, Cecil Cone, and others beginning in the 1960s.[94] It is a theology of, about, and by African Americans. And while the formal proponents of this theology were a group of creative Protestant, scholars, African American Catholic thinkers have used it as a point of departure to elaborate theological reflection that is both African American and Catholic.[95] The contributions made to this theology are decidedly significant, but what they have added to the discussion on the nature of authentic African American Catholic liturgy is invaluable.

79.   These theologians state that spirituality must be the starting point of a distinctively African American Catholic liturgy. It is a spirituality that is born of moments of the African American sense of "conversion." This conversion is neither "confected" nor produced in liturgy as much as it is nourished and sustained.[96]

80.   The African American bishops, in their pastoral letter *What We Have Seen And Heard*, spoke eloquently of some of the qualities of an African American spirituality. They called particular attention to its contemplative, holistic, joyful, and communitarian nature.

Contemplative

81. African American spirituality "senses the awe of God's transcendence and the vital intimacy of His closeness."[97] Lifted up into God's presence, African Americans respond by surrendering and basking completely in marvelous mystery, whether in church on bended knee or at home in labor or at rest. This contemplative prayer is central and pervasive in the African American tradition.

Holistic

82. African American spirituality involves the whole person: intellect and emotion, spirit and body, action and contemplation, individual and community, secular and sacred.

> In keeping with our African heritage, we are not ashamed of our emotions. For us, the religious experience is an experience of the whole human being, both the feeling and the intellect, the heart as well as the head. It is a spirituality grounded in the doctrine of the Incarnation—our belief that Jesus is both divine and human.[98]

It is a spirituality needed in a society that produces "progressive dehumanization brought about by a technocratic society."[99]

Joyful

83. African American spirituality explodes in the joy of movement, song, rhythm, feeling, color, and sensation. "This joy is a result of our conviction that 'in the time of trouble, He will lead me.' . . . This joy comes from the teaching and wisdom of our mothers and fathers in the Faith."[100]

Communitarian

84. African American spirituality means community. Worship is always a celebration of community. Because in this spirituality, "I" takes its meaning from "we"; "community means social concern for human suffering and other people's concerns."[101]

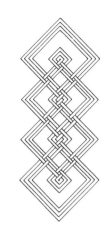

49

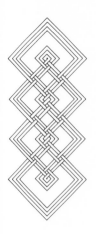

C. Emotion: A Way of Learning

85.   Third, the qualities of an African American spirituality suggest that this spirituality, which is deeply rooted in faith, has a strongly intuitive and emotive base. Nathan Jones, Jawanza Kunjufu, Alvin Pouissant, Na'im Akbar, and many others tell us that there are many ways of knowing and relating to the world.[102] The intellect is not the only way to experience reality. Reality may be experienced by emotion. Leopold Sedar Senghor expresses it best:

> The elan vital of Black Africans, their self-abandonment to the Other (e-motion) is, therefore, animated by reason — reason, note, that is not the reason of "seeing" of European whites, which is more a reason of set categories into which the outside world is forced. African reason is more *logos* (word) than *ratio* (intellect). For *ratio* is compasses, square and sextant, scale and yardstick, whereas *logos* is the living Word, the most specifically human expression of the neuro-sensorial impression . . . The Black African *logos* in its ascent to the *Verbum* (transcendent) removes the rust from reality to bring out its primordial color, grain, texture, sound, and color.[103]

This emotive way of knowing is not based primarily on the sense of sight as in the ocular, print-oriented culture of Europe, but on the African oral tradition, which tends to be poetic rather than literal.

86.   Whereas the European way might be summarized in Descartes' "I think, therefore, I am"; the African model might be "I am, I dance the Other, I am." For,

> Africans do not make a distinction between themselves and the Object, whether it be tree or stone, human or beast. . . . They become receptive to the impression it emanates, and, like the blind, take hold of it, full of life, with no attempt to hold it in store, without killing it. . . . Black Africans are children of the third day of creation, pure sensory fields.[104]

87.   Father Clarence Joseph Rivers, noted African American liturgist, informs us that in this way of knowing "there is a natural tendency for interpenetration and interplay, creating a concert or orchestration in which the ear sees, the eye hears, and where one both smells and tastes color; wherein all the

senses, unmuted, engage in every experience."[105] This way of knowing does not exclude a discursive dimension. It simply states that emotion is the primary way of knowing among African peoples and their descendants. It attests that objective detachment and analytical explanations are useful, but are not the sole means of communicating faith.[106] And lastly, it asserts that peoples everywhere are not poetic or discursive, but both poetic and discursive.

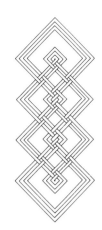

D. Some Ritual Emphases

88.   Fourth and finally, this articulated African American spirituality comes to full expression in ritual activity, that activity where the Creator and creation meet; where the assembled look upon the face of God and do not die but are sustained;[107] where special attention is paid to space, time, action, language, preaching, and song.

Space

89.   The hush-harbors, places of conversion and wholeness, of prayer and preaching, of solace and forgiveness, of shout and dance, were the places where the enslaved went to worship. It was in these small-group spaces that they responded to the God of their forebears in praise, adoration, and reverence. It was in these places that God brought healing, meaning, sustenance, and wholeness to them as individuals and as a group.[108] Today, the holy ground on which the African American assembly gathers, hears God's life-giving Word, gives thanks in a sacrificial meal, and is sent back into the world must be a hush-harbor. As in former times, these hush-harbors may be anywhere, but they must reflect the assembly whose roots are both African and American, not simply African or American. For as surely as the hush-harbors of old formed the assembly, our new African American liturgical environments will shape those worshiping today. And as the worshipers are shaped, so too is the world in which they live.

90.   The current hush-harbors must be "houses of the Church." They must be spaces that have "the power to anchor and map our human world and our Christian journey through it."[109] They must be places that give full sway to the rich array of the auditory, tactile, visual, and olfactory senses.[110] They must communicate relations with an African heritage and with the struggle of people today. They must be

places that speak clearly to the reality that here in this sacred space is an African American, Roman Catholic people gathered for the celebration of word and sacrament. Consequently, this space must be attentive to and mindful of not only all that the African American community has to say, but also of all that the Church has to say about environment as well, especially in chapters 5 and 6 of the *General Instruction of the Roman Missal* and the statement of the Bishops' Committee on the Liturgy, *Environment and Art in Catholic Worship.*

Time

91.   The expressions, ''We're going to have a good time'' and ''We're going to have church,'' sum up the African American's experience of sacred time. Although it is our duty and salvation always and everywhere to give thanks to God, gathering for liturgy is not simply an obligation. Gathering for liturgy is a time of glory and praise. Gathering for liturgy is ''passing time'' with the Lord. It is a time to heal the ''sin-sick'' soul. It is a time to give the Spirit breathing room. It is a time to tell the ancient story, at dawn and at dusk, on Sunday, and in every season. It is preeminently a time for the liturgical re-presentation of the paschal mystery: the dying and rising of Christ, that event of ''the life of Jesus of Nazareth, who was born, lived, taught, ministered, suffered, was put to death, transcended death paradoxically and was proclaimed and exalted as the Chirst. . . . [This event] is celebrated in liturgy in such a way that its interpretation of the past event has a plenitude of meaning for the present. That past event becomes sacred time.''[111]

Action

92.   Holy hands lifted in prayer, bowed heads, bended knee, jumping, dancing, and shouting were all accepted movements in ancient African American worship because they were creative (i.e., created by the Spirit, who moves us to do so) (see Rom 8:15). In an African American liturgy today, this movement must still play a vital part, not merely because it is a vestige of an African heritage but because gesture is a long-standing tradition of Roman Catholic worship as well.[112] Gestures reveal our inner feelings, hopes, fears, dreams, and longings for freedom. Furthermore:

> If we attend to our experience of bodily interaction with others, we discover that we become the persons we are

through that interaction. We learn from the caring touch of a parent that we are valued and loved, and that incites in us the ability to value and love others in return. The attentive, engrossed look on the face of a conversation partner encourages us to share and develop the feelings and ideas within us. The forgiving hug of a friend loosens in us an unsuspected power to forgive. A hand stretched out to us in a moment of need teaches us how to rise above self-concern in dealing with others. In other words, we are called forth to become the persons we are by the deeds of others.[113]

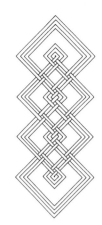

93. In both the Church and the African American community, there is great evidence of the power of posture in prayer.

Prayer said standing with head and hands upraised becomes prayer of praise and self-commitment. Bended knees and bowed head plead and repent. Raised hands speak of hearts lifted to God. A handshake or an embrace offers a peace which the world cannot give. Hands folded as mirror images of each other bring an inner quiet and peace of soul. Sitting hollows out in us a lap-like receptivity to receive a word in faith.[114]

94. Crying out soars to heaven and joins in the great seraphic hymn. Waving hands proclaim a deep-down praise and thanks when mere words fail. And being slain in the spirit brings an abiding and quickening rest to a world-weary soul. One caveat:

The liturgy of the Church has been rich in a tradition of ritual movement and gestures. These actions, subtly, yet really, contribute to an environment which can foster prayer or which can distract from prayer. When the gestures are done in common, they contribute to the unity of the worshiping assembly. Gestures which are broad and full in both a visual and tactile sense, support the entire symbolic ritual. When gestures are done by the presiding minister, they can either engage the entire assembly and bring them into even greater unity, or if done poorly, they can isolate.[115]

Language: Prayer

95. African American liturgy is marked by a rich narrative

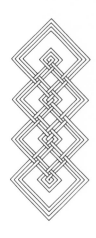

quality. Words are important. And how words are used in prayer is critical.

> Prayer in the Black Tradition is the very center of the Christian life of Black people and continues to be the basis of hope. In those days when they dwelt in the dark valley of bondage hope was yet unborn. It was through prayer in which they found solace and temporary escape from their sordid condition. . . . The prayers were so fervent, they seemed to ring up heaven. A significant and cogent feature of the prayers was the theological and sociological aspects. Their God was the same God of Abraham, Isaac, and Jacob; a captain who never lost a battle; a God of unrelenting love and forgiveness. Yet their prayers were always mindful of their brothers and sisters who shared some hope for freedom some day. . . . Today in an unsupportive society, prayer for Black people is still the "soul's sincere desire."[116]

96. The language of African American liturgy can be proclamatory in "witnessing" and attentive in listening; very personal without being exclusive; immanent while genuinely transcendent; exuberant and profoundly silent. It is a language that promotes the assembly's full active participation.[117]

Language: Preaching

97. Words are also important in the art of preaching. James Weldon Johnson has described the role of preaching in African American worship this way:

> The old-time Negro preacher was above all an orator, and in good measure, an actor. He knew the secret of oratory, that at bottom it is a progression of rhythmic words more than anything else. I have witnessed congregations moved to ecstasy by the rhythmic intonations. He was a master of all the modes of eloquence. He often possessed a voice that was a marvelous instrument, a voice he could modulate from a sepulchral whisper to a crashing thunderclap. His discourse was generally kept at a high pitch of fervency, but occasionally he dropped into colloquialisms and, less often, into humor. He preached a personal and anthropomorphic God, a sure-enough heaven and red-hot hell. His imagination was bold and unfettered. He had the power to sweep his hearers before him; and so he himself was often swept away. At such times his language was not prose but poetry.[118]

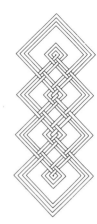

98. Preaching frequently becomes a dialogue involving the preacher and the assembly. When the preacher delivers a sermon or makes an important point, the congregation may respond from their hearts: "Amen!"; "Yes, Lord!"; "Thank you, Jesus!" They may hum. And sometimes worshipers may simply raise their hands on high in silent gestures of praise, gratitude, and affirmation. These responses are an acclamation of faith that neither demand nor expect any rubrics.

99. Because of the African American aesthetic appreciation of the vivid narrative form, the celebration of the Word of God in African American worship must be viewed as an experience of communal storytelling through which salvation history is related to the day-to-day lives of the faithful. The presiding minister is the leader of this storytelling experience. The presiding minister is a person of the "Book" (the Scriptures), whose role is to articulate the tale of the Christ event so that people can relate the salvation experience to their lives.[119]

100. Both preaching and praying are always in need of improvement. Those who are called to minister in the African American community must see it as their sacred trust to develop effective, spirit-filled, sound preaching and prayer. Both are a folk art. Thus, white and African American preacher-presiding ministers alike can benefit by learning more about the techniques of this African American liturgical art and regularly evaluating their ministry.

Sacred Song

101. The "soul" in African American liturgy calls forth a great deal of musical improvisation and creativity. It also calls forth a greater sense of spontaneity. The African American assembly is not a passive, silent, nonparticipating assembly. It participates by responding with its own interjections and acclamations, with expressions of approval and encouragement.

102. This congregational response becomes a part of the ritualized order of the celebration. The assembly has a sense of when and how to respond in ways that would no more disrupt the liturgy than applause would interrupt a politician's speech or laughter a comedian's monologue. The deadly silence of an unresponsive assembly gives the impression that the Spirit is absent from the community's act of praise.[120]

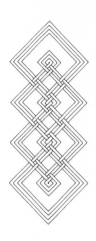

103.   African Americans are heirs to the West African musical aesthetic of the call-and-response structure, extensive melodic ornamentation (e.g., slides, slurs, bends, moans, shouts, wails, and so forth), complex rhythmic structures, and the integration of song and dance.[121] As a result, African American sacred song, as Thea Bowman noted, is:

holistic: challenging the full engagement of mind, imagination, memory, feeling, emotion, voice, and body;

participatory: inviting the worshiping community to join in contemplation, in celebration, and in prayer;

real: celebrating the immediate concrete reality of the worshiping community—grief or separation, struggle or oppression, determination or joy—bringing that reality to prayer within the community of believers;

spirit-filled: energetic, engrossing, intense; and

life-giving: refreshing, encouraging, consoling, invigorating, sustaining.[122]

African American sacred song is also the song of the people, a people "who share and claim a common history, a common experience, a common oppression, common values, hopes, dreams, and visions."[123]

104.   African American Catholic worship may be greatly enhanced by spirituals and gospel music, both of which are representations of this aesthetic. But classical music; anthems; African Christian hymns; jazz; South American, African-Caribbean, and Haitian music may also be used where appropriate. It is not just the style of music that makes it African American, but the African American assembly that sings it and the people whose spirits are uplifted by it.

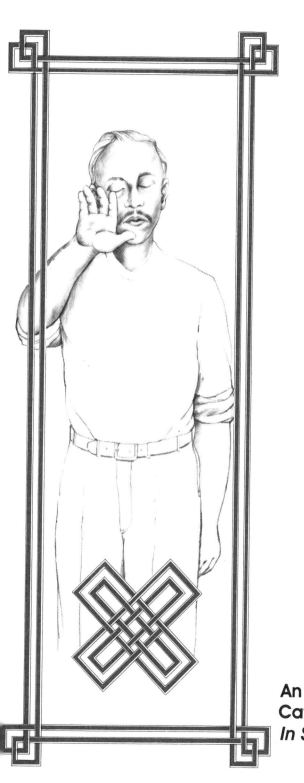

**An African American
Catholic Worship Model:**
In Spirit and Truth

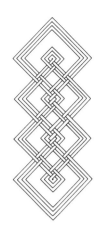

# n African American Catholic Worship Model
In Spirit and Truth

A. The Importance of Sunday Worship

105.   The one Church of Jesus Christ is indeed a home to us all, a place where all cultures meet and contribute to the one Body of Christ. The liturgy is the summit toward which the activity of this family (the Church) is directed; at the same time it is the fount from which all its power flows.[124] Of preeminence is the Church's Sunday Eucharist:

> For on this day Christ's faithful must gather together so that, by hearing the word of God and taking part in the eucharist, they may call to mind the passion, the resurrection, and the glorification of the Lord Jesus and may thank God, who "has begotten them again unto a living hope through the resurrection of Jesus Christ from the dead" (1 Pt 1:3).[125]

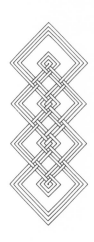

106. This Sunday celebration of the dying and rising of Christ has several principal requisites:

a. the gathering of the faithful to manifest the Church, not simply on their own initiative but as called together by God, that is, as the people of God in their organic structure, presided over by a priest, who acts in the person of Christ;

b. their instruction in the paschal mystery through the Scriptures that are proclaimed and that are explained by a priest or deacon;

c. the celebration of the eucharistic sacrifice, by which the paschal mystery is expressed, and which is carried out by the priest in the person of Christ and offered in the name of the entire Christian people.[126]

107. African American Catholics and those ministering with them are most sincerely thankful for and respectful of this Sunday liturgy. While realizing that the Church's eucharistic and sacramental tradition is not the same as that of the Protestant evangelical tradition, many African Americans recognize that a more caring celebration of the Roman Rite encourages a wedding of the Gospel of Jesus Christ and the rich heritage of the African American culture—a process in which the liturgy is not adapted to the culture as much as the liturgical assembly absorbing the best and most fitting cultural elements into itself in a rich diversity of ways and over long periods of time.[127]

108. Currently, there may be no worshiping community to which the Church in the United States can turn as an ideal example of authentic indigenous African American Catholic worship. One parish may have the appropriate balance of choir and congregational participation.[128] Another may have a powerful preaching tradition that does not eclipse an equally important liturgy of the Eucharist. Still another may have found ways to relate heroes from the larger African American experience with more traditional Catholic saints. Yet another may have found ways to respect the diversity of the African American worshiping community itself, taking care not to impose something on older people or younger people or Catholics from different parts of the country.

3. Principles of Cultural Adaptation

09.   Although no model worshiping community presently exists, there are principles, based on the very nature of the liturgy itself, that should guide those African Americans who are in the ardent search of such a model:[129]

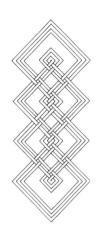

- ". . . the liturgy is above all things the worship of the divine majesty" (SC 33 [DOL 1]). It is humanity's personal encounter with God in faith, hope, and love through Christ in the community of the Church;

- Christ and his paschal mystery are at the very center of every liturgical act, whether the liturgy celebrates Baptism, or Eucharist, or the Liturgy of the Hours. The Church continually proclaims Christ and his salvific act of dying and rising;

- the Church prays through Christ, with Christ, and in Christ to God, the Father, in the union of the Holy Spirit;

- "the liturgy is made up of unchangeable elements divinely instituted (e.g., water for baptism, food and drink for eucharist), and elements subject to change" (signs dependent upon the culture and tradition of the people, e.g., the method used for the exchange of peace during the sign of peace);

- "Sacred Scripture is of the greatest importance in the celebration of the liturgy" (SC 24 [DOL 1]), that is, the Word of God is a sacramental that effects what it says. Therefore, non-biblical literature should not be used in the place of God's Word or in such a way as to draw the assembly's attention away from this Word;

- the assembly's full, conscious, and active participation in liturgical celebrations is called for by the very nature of the liturgy (SC 14 [DOL 1]), while respecting the simplicity of the rites and the varying roles of the liturgical ministers within these rites;

- there is an educative and catechetical value present in every liturgy, since each liturgy "contains rich instruction for the faithful. For in the liturgy God is speaking to his people and Christ is still proclaiming his Gospel" (SC 33 [DOL 1]);

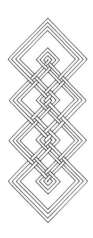

- the use of a language that reflects the thought of the people, native symbols, and motifs can help make signs and symbols clear.

C. *In Spirit and Truth*: A Model

110.   Though no model African American Catholic community exists, there is a signpost—based on a love of the Church's liturgy, an equal love of the powerful, religious traditions of the African American community, and the guidelines articulated above—that may assist in pointing the way to such a worshiping community. That signpost is *In Spirit and Truth: Black Catholic Reflections on the Order of Mass.*

111.   The Black Liturgy Subcommittee of the Bishops' Committee on the Liturgy prepared those reflections to assist and enhance the liturgical life of parish communities and to present the many opportunities already present for the accommodation of the liturgy to the "genius and talents" of the many ethnic, cultural, and racial groups that make up the Church in the United States, particularly the African American community.[130]

Preliminary Gathering

112.   Noting the long-standing traditions of "fellowship" and "witnessing" in the Black Church, *In Spirit and Truth* suggests a preliminary gathering:

> The purpose of this preliminary gathering is most commonly to help the congregation experience Christ's presence and to build up fellowship within the assembly. . . .[131]

Later, while discussing the sign of peace in the Communion Rite, *In Spirit and Truth* offers this reflection:

> The warmth and affection of Black Catholic communities may prompt the extension or enlargement of this ritual [the sign of peace] to the point that it overshadows the sharing of the Bread of Life, the richest sign of Christians' oneness in Christ. Extended greetings and signs of communicating affection are more properly given during the *Preliminary Gathering of the Assembly* and not at this time.[132]

113.   A preliminary gathering, presided over by a deacon or lay minister, might resemble the following:[133]

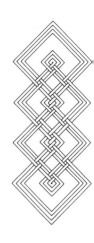

- An organ or choral prelude as the assembly gathers.

- A well-known congregational hymn that engenders a sense of fellowship or reflects the theme of that day's Scripture readings.

- A scriptural greeting and testimony.

   This is a time when many or a few members of the church stand and utter their praises to God for what God has done. This time need "not be eternal to be immortal (see Mt 6:7-8). It lifts people from the habit of rote prayers, and it causes them to say in one or two lines exactly the thought they would utter to God."[134]

   As an example, the presiding minister might say:

   > They that hope in the Lord
   > Will renew their strength,
   > They will soar as with eagles' wings;
   > They will run and not grow weary,
   > Walk and not grow faint (Is 40:31).

   > What a mighty God we serve! Amen? Amen!
   > Is there anyone who wishes to witness to the Lord's goodness this morning?

   One who gives testimony might say:

   > Saints of God, I have been coming up the rough side of the mountain all week. Along the way I thought I wouldn't make it. But I kept on praying, and the Lord has brought me through. He has made a way out of no way, and I am here to tell the story! Amen!

   or:

   > This week has been a particularly rough one for me, my friends. But I have survived because the Lord is truly like a mother who forgets not her child. And I'm so glad that God has not forgotten me.

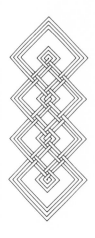

- A prayer.

  After the leader has discerned that the testimonies should come to an end,[135] he or she may collect all these praises into one prayer, summarizing the concerns of those who have spoken.

- Fellowship.

  This is a time when those who form the assembly may greet one another enthusiastically.[136]

  For example, the leader might say:

  > The Lord's kindness never fails. Let us ready ourselves to receive that kindness in abundance. Let us stand and greet one another in fellowship, for this is the day the Lord has made. Let us rejoice and be glad!

This preliminary gathering may also take the form of hymn singing, catechesis, instruction for the liturgy, and fellowship.

Prayer

114.   Recalling the African American community's rich tradition of prayer, *In Spirit and Truth* states:

> The invitation *Let us pray* is always addressed to the assembly and never to God. This invitation may be extended and adapted to the needs of the assembly, in the style of alternative opening prayers found in the *Sacramentary*. Any variation in this invitation should focus upon the opening prayer prescribed for the day, which must always be said. . . .[137]

Compare:

> Let us pray
> [to the Father whose kindness never fails]
> (Eighteenth Sunday in Ordinary Time)

with:

> Let us pray
> to the Father whose kindness never fails.
> Let us pray
> to the God of our salvation.

Let us pray
for peace and life and guidance
on our pilgrim way.

or:

Our God is good, yes? Yes! Amen!
Our God is gracious, yes? Yes! Amen!
Our God has helped us, yes? Yes! Amen!
Helped us travel this lonesome valley, yes? Yes! Amen!
Then let us open our hearts and bow our heads
And pray to our God whose kindness never fails.[138]

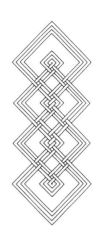

115. The penitential rite and the general intercessions are
additional opportunities for using the beauty and poetry of
African American prayer to great effect:[139]

A Possible Penitential Rite for
the Eighteenth Sunday in Ordinary Time, Sunday Cycle A[140]

Priest or Deacon:
Mindful of our many sins
and hungering for forgiveness,
let us remember God's mercy
made manifest in Christ Jesus our Lord.
(pause)

Lord Jesus Christ, you are our Bread of heaven, Lamb of
God and Word of life. Lord, have mercy.

Lord Jesus Christ, you are our Rock in a weary land, and
our Shelter in the storm. Christ, have mercy.

Lord Jesus Christ, you are our soon-coming King. Lord,
have mercy.

A Possible Litany for the General Intercessions for
the Eighteenth Sunday in Ordinary Time, Sunday Cycle A[141]

Priest:
O brothers and sisters,
drawn together by Jesus, the Bread of Life,
and mindful of God's manifold blessings,
we cry out that the many hungers of the world
may indeed be satisfied.

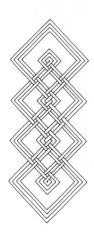

Minister:

For the Church scattered throughout the world and longing to spread the Good News of God's most merciful reign, we pray to the Lord. Lord, have mercy.

For our elected leaders who labor for an abiding justice and a peace unending, we pray to the Lord. Lord, have mercy.

For the homeless who ache for shelter, the poor who hunt for bread, the young who starve for love, we pray to the Lord. Lord, have mercy.

For the broken in mind and body who set their hearts on wholeness, especially those for whom we now pray (pause to allow the congregation to voice names of the sick), we pray to the Lord. Lord, have mercy.

For the dead who yearn for eternal rest, especially those for whom we now pray (pause to allow the congregation to voice names of the dead), we pray to the Lord. Lord, have mercy.

Priest:

Heavenly Father,
hear us in what we ask
and perfect us in what we do
and, at last, gather us into your kingdom
where our deepest needs will be satisfied
through Christ our Lord.

Scripture

116. Keeping in mind the African American community's unbroken love of Scripture, *In Spirit and Truth* observes:

"In the dark days of slavery, reading was forbidden, but for our ancestors the Bible was never a closed book. The stories were told and retold in sermons, spirituals and shouts, proverbs and turns of phrases borrowed freely from the Bible. . . . Thus, when the word of Scripture is proclaimed in the Black community, it is not a new message but a new challenge" (*What We Have Seen And Heard*, pp. 4-5). . . .

. . . [Consequently] a reader may, according to his or her talent, lend a spirit of enthusiasm to the proclamation of the Scripture texts. Many Black Americans have long grown accustomed to such a spirited proclamation of God's word. So long as the word of God is announced with faith, clarity, and sincerity such styles may be appropriate in the Eucharist.[142]

Homily

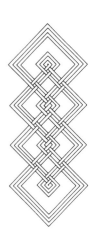

117. Acknowledging the fertile past of the African American preaching, *In Spirit and Truth* reminds us:

[T]he homily is an application of the Scripture readings and the meaning of the solemnity or feast to everyday Christian living and continued conversion.
   The style and manner of preaching should be influenced by "the composition and expectations of the congregation to which it is addressed and not exclusively by the preference of the preacher" (see Bishops' Committee on Priestly Life and Ministry, *Fulfilled in Your Hearing: The Homily in the Sunday Assembly*, p. 25:1). . . .
   . . . Traditionally, good "Black preaching" is rich in content and expression, relies heavily on the biblical text, and draws generously from story, song, poetry, humor, anecdote, and descriptive language. Good Black preaching balances emotion and content and never descends to crass affectation. . . .[143]

Liturgy of the Eucharist

118. Remembering the African American community's longing for continual conversion, its desire to stand at the foot of the cross, and the zeal of souls who sing "How great Thou art!" beckons the community to gather around the table of the Lord.[144] *In Spirit and Truth* remarks:[145]

"At the last supper Christ instituted the sacrifice and paschal meal that make the sacrifice of the cross to be continuously present in the Church, when the priest, representing Christ the Lord, carries out what the Lord did and handed over to his disciples to do in his memory" (*General Instruction of the Roman Missal*, 48). . . .
   The eucharistic prayer, also called the anaphora, "a prayer of thanksgiving and sanctification, is the center of the entire celebration" (Bishops' Committee on the Liturgy, *Music in Catholic Worship*, 47).

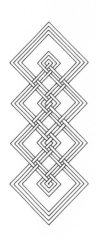

Sacred Song

119.   Observing the African American community's character-istic for dialogue and acclamation, and its passion for singing the Lord's song, *In Spirit and Truth* urges the examination of the use of music:[146]

● in the Entrance Song;

● at the Gloria;

● as the assembly prepares to hear God's word;

● in the Responsorial Psalm;

● at the Gospel procession;

● after the proclamation of the Gospel;

● in the General Intercessions;

● at the Preparation of the Altar and the Gifts;

● for the acclamations in the Eucharistic Prayer;

● for the Lord's Prayer;[147]

● at the Breaking of the Bread;

● for the Communion procession;

● for the Psalm or Hymn of Praise after Communion; and

● at the Recessional.

Gesture

120.   Understanding the African American community's af-fection for gesture, *In Spirit and Truth* points out those places where gesture and other movements are appropriate:[148]

● the Entrance Procession;

● the Gospel Procession;

● the Preparation of the Altar and the Gifts;

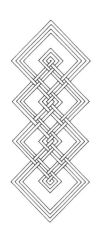

- the Communion Rite;[149] and

- the Recessional.

Silence

121.   Appreciating the African American community's sense of profound silence, *In Spirit and Truth* calls to mind the liturgy's call to silence:[150]

- during the Opening Prayer and Prayer after Communion; and

- after Communion.

The liturgical celebration will be served by this additional reminder:

> Silence should be observed at the designated times as part of the celebration. Its function depends on the time it occurs in each part of the celebration. Thus at the penitential rite and again after the invitation to pray, all recollect themselves; at the conclusion of a reading or the homily, all meditate briefly on what has been heard; after communion, all praise God in silent prayer (*General Instruction of the Roman Missal*, 23 [DOL 208]).

Welcoming of Guests

122.   Finally, as was noted earlier, fellowship and hospitality are a fundamental element of the Black Church experience. One manifestation of that hospitality is the warm attention paid to visitors and guests. In many Black churches where this tradition survives, the welcoming of guests is an important part of the pastor's announcements.[151] In keeping with that tradition and noting the placement of announcements at the beginning of the Concluding Rites of the Sunday liturgy,[152] we might suggest the following as one of those brief announcements:

> Mindful of the Lord's words:
> "Anyone who welcomes you welcomes me," (Mt 10:40)
> we welcome all our guests.
> To those of you who are Catholic
> and have no church home,

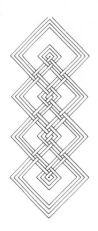

please feel free to see me or one of our ushers
about becoming an active member of our church family.
To those of you who may possibly be seeking membership
in the Catholic Church, please see me
about initiating so wondrous a step.
Again, know that you are all welcome.

D. Conclusion

123.   *In Spirit and Truth* provides an excellent model and
serves as a worthy signpost. But it must be remembered that
African American Catholics are in the process of developing
and continuing a tradition, a laudatory and difficult task.[153]
This task is one in which we welcome from the African American culture all that is "compatible with aspects of the true
and authentic spirit of the liturgy, in respect for the substantial unity of the Roman Rite."[154] This task, as John Paul II reminds us, ". . . demands a serious formation in theology, history, and culture as well as a sound judgment in discerning
what is necessary or useful and what is not useful or even
dangerous to faith. . . ."[155] It will take time for people who are
authentically African American and truly Catholic and who
know the nature of the liturgy and worship to nurture this
tradition. In the meantime, African American Catholics must
establish, with the authority of the Congregation for Divine
Worship and the Discipline of the Sacraments, the Bishops'
Committee on the Liturgy, and their local bishops, various liturgical centers of pastoral sensitivity and academic excellence
where liturgists, scholars, artists, musicians, and pastors may
continue to dedicate their skills in God's service.[156] Furthermore, these prayerful men and women might do well to look
beyond these shores to Africa. As Bishop Wilton D. Gregory
has exhorted:

> It might well be and in many cases I suspect that it will
> be true that there is much that the Church in service to
> African Americans can learn from and use from the Cath-
> olic Church in Africa. Our people need to continue to ex-
> plore the genuine and authentic African heritage that is
> ours, but has been denied or denigrated for far too long.
> What we do not need are facile, inaccurate, incomplete,
> uninformed exposure to certain African traditions which
> ignore the complexity of their origin used in a Catholic
> ritual context without proper explanation and reverence
> for either the ritual or African custom.[157]

124. And finally, African Americans all must pray:

> Be in the fleeting word, our Father, the stumbling effort.
> Touch mind and heart and life,
> that as we move from this place
> into the way that we must take,
> we shall not be alone,
> but feel Thy Presence beside us, all the way.[158]

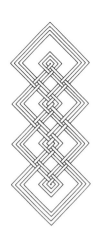

African Americans must pray so as to continue exploring and searching the established traditions of the Church and the powerful gifts of the African American culture, in order to determine what is the best result for the Church—all to the greater honor and glory of God, in whose house there is plenty good room!

End notes

Introduction

1. Cf. Second Vatican Ecumenical Council, *Pastoral Constitution on the Church in the Modern World, Gaudium et Spes* [= GS] (December 7, 1965), 1 [*Documents on the Liturgy, 1963–1979: Conciliar, Papal, and Curial Texts* = DOL, 19].

2. Cf. GS 1 [DOL 19].

3. See GS 53-62 [DOL 19].

4. Cf. *Handbook of the National Conference of Catholic Bishops/ United States Catholic Conference* (Washington, D.C.: USCC Office for Publishing and Promotion Services, 1989), 1e, p. 56.

5. See John Paul II, "Meeting with Black Catholic Leadership" (September 12, 1987, New Orleans, La.) in *Unity in the Work of Service* (Washington, D.C.: USCC Office for Publishing and Promotion Services, 1987), pp. 51-55.

6. See Second Vatican Ecumenical Council, *Constitution on the Liturgy, Sacrosanctum Concilium* [= SC] (December 4, 1963), 37-40 [DOL 1].

Text

1. Saint Augustine, Confessions 1,i,1.

2. Cf. Eucharistic Prayer IV; Psalms 145:16 and 136:25.

3. Coretta Scott King, ed., *The Words of Martin Luther King, Jr.* (New York: Newmarket Press, 1987), p. 64.

4. Cf. Joseph Gelineau, SJ, *Liturgy: Today and Tomorrow* (New York: Paulist Press, 1978).

5. Gilbert Ostdiek, OFM, *Catechesis for Liturgy* (Washington, D.C.: The Pastoral Press, 1986), p. 50.

6. Cf. Mircea Eliade, *The Sacred and the Profane* (New York: Harper Torchbook, 1959).

7. Howard Thurman, *The Growing Edge* (Richmond, Ind.: Friends United Press, 1956), p. 117.

8. For an extensive explanation of symbol, see Edward K. Braxton, "Reflections from a Theological Perspective," *This Far by Faith: American Black Catholic Worship and Its African Roots* (Washington, D.C.: The Liturgical Conference, 1977).

9. Cf. *Catechesis for Liturgy*.

10. Cf. Sean Swayne, *Gather Around the Lord: A Vision for Renewal of the Sunday Eucharist* (Dublin, Ireland: The Columba Press, 1987), pp. 32-36.

11. Cf. Saint John Chrysostom, *Homilies on the Gospel of Matthew*, Matthew 14:23-24, no. 50, para. 3-4.

12. Cf. Paul Ricoeur, *The Symbolism of Evil* (Boston: Beacon Press, 1967).

13. Cf. *Liturgy: Today and Tomorrow*.

14. *Catechesis for Liturgy*, pp. 13-20.

15. Cf. Braxton, *This Far by Faith*, p. 74.

16. Saint Augustine, *Sermon on the Words of the Gospel*, Luke 7:2, para. 1.

17. Cf. Eucharistic Prayer III; Acts 2:33.

18. Cf. Eucharistic Prayer IV; Romans 12:1, Ephesians 1:14.

19. Cf. *Gather Around the Lord*, pp. 12-20.

20. Cf. Anscar J. Chupungco, OSB, *Cultural Adaptation of the Liturgy* (New York: Paulist Press, 1982), p. 7.

21. Cf. Theodor Klauser, *A Short History of the Western Liturgy* (Oxford: Oxford University Press, 1979), pp. 4-7.

22. Cf. ibid., p. 7.

23. Cf. *Cultural Adaptation of the Liturgy*, p. 11.

24. Cf. *A Short History of the Western Liturgy*, pp. 30-32. This custom of praying through, with, and in Christ is one that is practiced and reaffirmed even to this day:

Christ Jesus, High Priest of the new and eternal covenant, taking human nature, introduced into this earthly exile the hymn that is sung throughout all ages in the halls of heaven. He joins the entire human community to himself, associating it with his own singing of this canticle of divine praise (SC 83).

Or in short:

Jesus sings the only song that is heard in heaven; those whose voices would be heard must sing along with Christ (Austin Fleming, *Preparing for Liturgy* [Washington, D.C.: The Pastoral Press, 1985], p. 17).

25. Cf. *Cultural Adaptation of the Liturgy*, pp. 20-22. Father Chupungco provides early definitions of *acculturation* and *inculturation*. Acculturation is "the process whereby cultural elements that are compatible with Roman Liturgy are incorporated into it either as substitutes for or illustrations of ritual elements of the Roman Rite. Inculturation is "the process whereby a pre-Christian rite is permanently given a Christian meaning" (Ibid., pp. 81-86). In a later work *Liturgies of the Future: The Process and Methods of Inculturation* (Mahwah, N.J.: Paulist Press, 1989), Father Chupungco further develops these definitions.

26. Cf. ibid., pp. 27-29.

27. Cf. Joseph P. Fitzpatrick, SJ, *One Culture Many Cultures: Challenge of Diversity* (Kansas City, Mo.: Sheed and Ward, 1987), pp. 54-61.

28. Pope Gregory the Great addressed a similar theme in his letter to Augustine of Canterbury:

You, brother, know the usage of the Roman Church in which you were brought up: hold it very much in affection. But as far as I am concerned, if you have found something more pleasing to Almighty God, either in the Frankish or in any other Church, make a careful choice and institute in the Church of the English—which as yet is new to the faith—the best usages which you have gathered together from many Churches. For we should love things not because of the places where they are found, but because of the good things they contain. Therefore choose from each particular Church what is godly, religious and sound, and gathering all together as it were into a dish, place it on the table of the English for their customary diet (*Cultural Adaptation of the Liturgy*, p. 26).

29. *A Short History of the Western Liturgy*, p. 2.

30. Cf. David A. Novak, "A Brief History of the Eucharist," Address to Eucharistic Ministers in the Diocese of Cleveland (November 12, 1989).

31. Walter Howard Frere, *The Anaphora or Great Eucharistic Prayer* (London: SPCK Press, 1938), p. 138.

32. Cf. *A Short History of the Western Liturgy*, pp. 117-123.

33. Cf. *One Culture Many Cultures*, pp. 61-91.

34. Cf. *A Short History of the Western Liturgy*, pp. 135-140.

35. *Cultural Adaptation of the Liturgy*, p. 34.

36. Cf. *A Short History of the Western Liturgy*, p. 122.

37. Cf. *Cultural Adaptation of the Liturgy*, pp. 37-38.

38. SC 26 [DOL 1].

39. SC 37 [DOL 1].

40. Cf. SC 38 [DOL 1].

41. Cf. SC 39 [DOL 1].

42. ". . . 'Missions' is the name generally given to those special undertakings by which heralds of the Gospel sent by the Church and going out into the whole world fulfill the office of preaching the Gospel and of implanting the Church among peoples or groups not yet believing in Christ" (Second Vatican Ecumenical Council, *Decree on the Church's Missionary Activity Ad Gentes Divinitus* [December 7, 1965], 6 [DOL 17]). According to this definition, would not "unchurched" African Americans be considered a valid mission?

43. SC 40 [DOL 1].

44. SC 48 [DOL 1].

45. Secretariat of State, "Letter of Cardinal Jean Villot to

Bishop R. Alberti, President of the Department of Liturgy of CELAM," On the Occasion of the Second Latin American Meeting on the Liturgy (Caracas, July 12-14, 1977), *Notitiae* 13 (1977): 459-467 [DOL 66].

46. Paul VI, "Address at the Closing of the Symposium of African Bishops Given at Kampala," Excerpt on the Liturgy and Different Cultures (July 31, 1969), AAS 61 (1969): 573-578 [DOL 44].

47. Cf. Clarence Joseph Rivers on the definition of "soul" in *Soulfull Worship* (Washington, D.C.: National Office for Black Catholics, 1974), p. 14.

48. These statements and pastoral letters are contained in the four-volume *Pastoral Letters of the United States Bishops, 1792-1983* (Washington, D.C.: USCC Office for Publishing and Promotion Services, 1984).

49. Joseph L. Howze, et al., *What We Have Seen and Heard: A Pastoral Letter on Evangelization from the Black Bishops of the United States* [= WWHSH] (Cincinnati: St. Anthony Messenger Press, 1984).

50. "Meeting with Black Catholic Leadership," *Unity in the Work of Service*, p. 55.

51. Cf. John Tracy Ellis, *American Catholicism* (Chicago: The University of Chicago Press, 1956), pp. 1-39; Dennis R. Clark, *Our Catholic Roots* (New York: Sadlier-Oxford, 1988), pp. 2-27.

52. For a discussion of the relationship between religion and culture see Bernard J. F. Lonergan, SJ, *Method in Theology* (New York: Herder and Herder, 1972).

53. WWHSH, p. 4.

54. Cf. John S. Mbiti, *African Religions and Philosophy* (New York: Praeger, 1970).

55. Cf. for example, ibid., pp. 100-162.

56. Cf. ibid., p. 108.

57. Cf. J. S. Mbiti, *Concepts of God in Africa* (New York: Praeger, 1970), pp. 1-154.

58. Cf. Diana L. Hayes, "Black Catholic Revivalism: The Emergence of a New Form of Worship," *The Journal of the Interdenominational Theological Center* XIV:1-2 (Fall 1986/Spring 1987): 87-107.

59. Cf. Gayraud S. Wilmore, *Black Religion and Black Radicalism*, Second Edition (New York: Orbis Books, 1983), p. 15.

60. Ibid., p. 16.

61. Cf. Charles B. Copher, "Biblical Characters, Events, Places, and Images Remembered and Celebrated in Black Church Worship," *The Journal of the Interdenominational Theological Center* XIV:1-2 (Fall 1986/Spring 1987): 75-86.

62. See *Songs of Zion* [= SOZ] (Nashville: Abingdon Press, 1981), no. 140.

63. See *Lead Me, Guide Me: The African American Catholic Hymnal* [= LMGM] (Chicago: GIA Publications, Inc., 1987), no. 318.

64. See LMGM, no. 292.

65. See LMGM, no. 293.

66. James H. Cone, *The Spirituals and the Blues: An Interpretation* (New York: Seabury Press, 1972), p. 54.

67. This strength in times of adversity is true even today:

> Recognizing the necessity for suffering I have tried to make it a virtue. If only to save myself from bitterness. . . . I have lived these last few years with the conviction that unearned suffering is redemptive. . . . So like the Apostle Paul, I can now humbly yet proudly say, "I bear in my body the marks of the Lord Jesus." The suffering and agonizing moments through which I have passed over the last few years have also drawn me closer to God. More than ever before, I am convinced of the reality of a personal God (Dr. Martin Luther King, Jr. in an interview with the *Christian Century* [April 27, 1960] as quoted in James M. Washington, *A Testament of Hope: The Essential Writings of Martin Luther King, Jr.* [San Francisco: Harper and Row, 1986], p. 41).

68. E. Franklin Frazier, *The Negro in America* (New York: Schocken Books, 1974), p. 23.

69. Catherine L. Albanese, *America: Religions and Religion* (Belmont, Calif.: Wadsworth Publishing Company, 1981), p. 120.

70. Cf. ibid., pp. 119-123.

71. *The Negro in America*, p. 24.

72. Cf. Clifton H. Johnson, ed., *God Struck Me Dead: Religious Conversion Experiences and Autobiographies of Ex-Slaves* (Philadelphia: Pilgrim Press, 1969).

73. Cf. James H. Cone, *The Spirituals and the Blues.*

74. See LMGM, no. 53.

75. See SOZ, no. 106.

76. See SOZ, no. 170.

77. See LMGM, no. 43.

78. See SOZ, no. 158.

79. See SOZ, no. 102.

80. See LMGM, no. 319.

81. See LMGM, nos. 107, 216.

82. Cf. Cyprian Davis, OSB, "Black Catholics in Nineteenth-Century America," *U.S. Catholic Historian* 5:1 (1986): 4-17.

83. See George Ofori-atta-Thomas, "African Inheritance in the Black Church Worship," *The Journal of the Interdenominational Theological Center* XIV:1-2 (Fall 1986/Spring 1987): 43-74. See also W. E. B. Du Bois, *The Gift of Black Folk* (Greenwich, Conn.: Fawcett, 1903); and Albert J. Raboteau, *Slave Religion* (Oxford: Oxford University Press, 1978).

84. See Robert C. Williams, "Worship and Anti-Structure in Thurman's Vision of the Sacred," *The Journal of the Interdenominational Theological Center* XIV:1-2 (Fall 1986/Spring 1987): 173. See also Robert Farris Thompson, *Flash of the Spirit* (New

York: Vintage Books, 1983); and Ulysses D. Jenkins, *Ancient African Religion and the African-American Church* (Jacksonville, N.C.: Flame International, 1978).

85. See O. Richard Bowyer, Betty L. Hart, Charlotte A. Meade, eds., *Prayer in the Black Tradition* (Nashville: The Upper Room, 1986).

86. Cf. Henry H. Mitchell, *Black Preaching* (San Francisco: Harper and Row, 1979).

87. Ibid., pp. 196-271.

88. See SOZ, no. 119.

89. See LMGM, no. 4.

90. See LMGM, no. 426.

91. *God Struck Me Dead*, p. 2.

92. See J-Glenn Murray, SJ, "The Liturgy of the Roman Rite and African American Worship," in LMGM.

93. Donald M. Clark, as cited in Bishop James P. Lyke, OFM, "Liturgical Expression in the Black Community," *Worship* 57:1 (January 1983): 20.

94. Cf. Eric Lincoln, *The Black Church Since Frazier* (New York: Schocken, 1974).

95. Cf. Gayraud S. Wilmore and James H. Cone, eds., *Black Theology: A Documented History* (Maryknoll, N.Y.: Orbis Books, 1979).

96. Cf. *Preparing for Liturgy*, p. 82.

97. WWHSH, p. 8.

98. Ibid.

99. Ibid., p. 9.

100. Ibid.

101. Ibid., p. 10.

102. Cf. Nathan Jones, *Sharing the Old, Old Story: Educational Ministry in the Black Community* (Winona, Minn.: Saint Mary's Press, 1982); Jawanza Kunjufu, *Developing Positive Self-Images and Discipline in Black Children* (Chicago: African-American Images, 1984); Alvin F. Pouissant, *Why Blacks Kill Blacks* (New York: Emerson Hall Publishers, 1972); Na'im Akbar, *Chains and Images of Psychological Slavery* (Jersey City: New Mind Productions, 1984); Reginald Lanier Jones, *Black Psychology* (New York; Harper and Row, 1972); and Alfred B. Pasteur and Ivory L. Toldson, *Roots of Soul: The Psychology of Black Expressiveness* (New York: Anchor Press, 1982).

103. Leopold Sedar Senghor, "The Psychology of the African Negro," *Freeing the Spirit*, as cited in Clarence Joseph Rivers, "The Oral African Tradition versus the Ocular Western Tradition," *This Far by Faith*, p. 41.

104. Ibid.

105. "The Oral African Tradition," p. 45.

106. See ibid., p. 49.

107. Cf. *Preparing for Liturgy*, p. 19.

108. Cf. Edward P. Wimberly, "The Dynamics of Black Worship: A Psychological Exploration of the Impulses that Lie at the Roots of Black Worship," *The Journal of the Interdenominational Theological Center* XIV:1-2 (Fall 1986/Spring 1987): 198.

109. *Catechesis for Liturgy*, p. 70.

110. Cf. Bishops' Committee on the Liturgy, National Conference of Catholic Bishops, *Environment and Art in Catholic Worship* [= EACW] (Washington, D.C.: USCC Office for Publishing and Promotion Services, 1978), 12.

111. "Reflections from a Theological Perspective," p. 74.

112. Cf. EACW 56.

113. *Catechesis for Liturgy*, p. 126.

114. Ibid., p. 128.

115. EACW 56.

116. *Prayer in the Black Tradition*, pp. 13-14.

117. Cf. SC 30.

118. James Weldon Johnson, *God's Trombones: Seven Negro Sermons in Verse* (New York: The Viking Press, 1969), p. 5.

119. Cf. Giles Conwill, "Black Preaching and Catholicism," *Ministry among Black Americans* (Indianapolis: Lilly Endowment, Inc., 1980), pp. 31-43.

120. "To promote active participation, the people should be encouraged to take part by means of acclamations, responses, psalmody, antiphons, and songs, as well as by actions, gestures, and bearing. And at the proper times all should observe a reverent silence" (SC 30) [DOL 1].

121. Cf. Portia K. Maultsby, "The Use and Performance of Hymnody, Spirituals and Gospels in the Black Church," *The Journal of the Interdenominational Theological Center* XIV:1-2 (Fall 1986/Spring 1987): 141-160.

122. See Thea Bowman, FSPA, "The Gift of African American Sacred Song," in LMGM, p. 3.

123. Ibid., p. 5.

124. Cf. SC 10 [DOL 1].

125. SC 106 [DOL 1].

126. Congregation for Divine Worship, *Directory for Sunday Celebrations in the Absence of a Priest* (June 2, 1988) ICEL trans. (Washington, D.C.: USCC Office for Publishing and Promotion Services, 1988), 12.

127. Cf. Aidan Kavanagh, OSB, *Elements of Rite: A Handbook of Liturgical Style* (New York: Pueblo Publishing Company, 1982), pp. 55-57.

128. Cf. J. Wendell Mapson, Jr., *The Ministry of Music in the Black Church* (Valley Forge: Judson Press, 1984), pp. 43-54.

129. *Cultural Adaptation of the Liturgy*, pp. 63-74.

130. Cf. Bishops' Committee on the Liturgy, National Confer-

ence of Catholic Bishops, *In Spirit and Truth: Black Catholic Reflections on the Order of Mass* [= IST] (Washington, D.C.: USCC Office for Publishing and Promotion Services, 1987), Preface, p. 1.

131. IST 9.

132. IST 51.

133. Cf. J-Glenn Murray, SJ, "Enfleshing *In Spirit and Truth*," Address Given to the African American Catholic Liturgical Ministers (Los Angeles, February 18, 1988).

134. Harold A. Carter, *The Prayer Tradition of Black People* (Valley Forge: Judson Press, 1976), p. 123.

135. Cf. ibid., p. 123.

136. "I advanced towards the people. The church was full. Cries of joy echoed through it: 'Glory to God! God be praised!' Nobody was silent. Shouts were coming from everywhere. I greeted the people, and again they began to cry out in their enthusiasm. Finally, when silence was restored the readings from the Sacred Scripture were proclaimed" (Saint Augustine, *The City of God*, 22, vii, 22, as cited in R. Cable, *The Church at Prayer*, vol. 2 [London: Geoffrey Chapman, 1986], p. 50).

137. IST 22.

138. "Enfleshing *In Spirit and Truth*."

139. Cf. IST 17, 18, 39-40.

140. "Enfleshing *In Spirit and Truth*."

141. Ibid.

142. IST 23, 26.

143. IST 33-35.

144. See Stuart K. Hine, "How Great Thou Art," in LMGM, no. 181.

145. IST 41, 44.

146. See IST 11, 20, 24, 28, 30, 32, 40, 42, 45, 49, 55, 57, 58, 59, 65.

147. Musical settings of the Lord's Prayer should always include the embolism ("Deliver us, Lord . . ."), a development of the last petition of the Lord's Prayer that begs, on behalf of the entire community of the faithful, deliverance from the power of evil (General Instruction, *Roman Missal* [= GIRM], 56a [DOL 208]. Given the times of great anxiety in which we live, this embolism surely needs to be prayed.

148. See IST 12-13, 31, 43, 66.

149. It might be suggested that the assembly stand in *orans* for the Lord's Prayer (see Tertullian, *De oratione,* 14), embrace at the Sign of Peace (GIRM 56b [DOL 208]), and make a proper reverence before the reception of Communion (GIRM 244c [DOL 208]).

150. See IST 21, 60.

151. Cf. Rawn Harbor, "Music and the Black Church Experience," Talk Given at the Black Catholic Worship Conference (Archdiocese of Detroit, February 3, 1989).

152. Cf. GIRM 123 [DOL 208].

153. Cf. Bishop Wilton D. Gregory, "Black Catholic Liturgy: What Do You Say It Is?" *U.S. Catholic Historian* 7:2-3 (Spring/Summer 1988): 316-319.

154. John Paul II, Apostolic Letter *On the Twenty-Fifth Anniversary of the "Constitution on the Sacred Liturgy"* (December 4, 1988) (Washington, D.C.: USCC Office for Publishing and Promotion Services, 1989), 16.

155. Ibid.

156. Cf. WWHSH, pp. 30-33.

157. Bishop Wilton D. Gregory, "Children of the Same Mother," Talk Given at the Workshop for Pastors Serving in the African American Catholic Community (Atlanta, May 12, 1990), pp. 11-12.

158. *The Growing Edge,* p. 154.